THE SPIRITUAL CONNECTION

EXPLORE YOUR TRUE POTENTIAL THROUGH A SPIRITUALLY CENTERED LIFE

BY: ASHLEIGH BENSON

ISBN 978-0-578-80021-9 (Hardcover Edition)

Library of Congress Cataloging-in-Publication Data is available upon request.

Cover Graphics/Art Credit: Duane Redwolf Miles and ArtofFrequency.com

Printed and Bound in the United States of America by Lulu

First Printing November 2020

Email: healer@Mystic-Oasis.com

Visit www.Mystic-Oasis.com

I dedicate this book to my beautiful children: Bobbi, Amanda, Beren and my family and friends who have encouraged me to never give up.

Table of Contents

Foreword
Introduction

Section 1: What is Spirituality   1
    Chapter 1: History of Spirituality   3
    Chapter 2: Elements of Spirituality   12
    Chapter 3: Importance of Spirituality   23
    Chapter 4: Spiritual Journey   26

Section 2: Knowing God/Holy Spirit   33
    Chapter 5: God/Holy Spirit   35
    Chapter 6: God's Attributes   44
    Chapter 7: The Character of God   53
    Chapter 8: God Sent Angels   65

Section 3: Personal Growth   79
    Chapter 9: Faith/Belief   81
    Chapter 10: True Self   95
    Chapter 11: Vibrational Energy   100
    Chapter 12: Chakras   108
    Chapter 13: Focus   115
    Chapter 14: Humility   121
    Chapter 15: Prayer/Meditation   124
    Chapter 16: Bible Study   129

Section 4: Full of Blessings   135
    Chapter 17: Blessings   137
    Chapter 18: Finances   141

About the Author

Foreword

Over the years, my family has patiently watched me writing. I always have a notebook nearby so I can jot down my thoughts. I believe our deepest thoughts are messages to share or act upon given to us by God, the universe, angels, and guides. They seem to come out of nowhere - a realization, an answer to a question, even a solution to a problem.

I am so thankful my friends and family urged me to compile all my notes and write this book. They are my biggest cheerleaders and supporters.

I genuinely hope you get as much enjoyment out of this book as I have had writing it.

Introduction

Everywhere you turn, there is strife, from the different government parties fighting amongst each other to different cultures - dissension is abundant. We can subtly change the negativity, struggle, and conflict around us by focusing on a higher spiritual connection.

You will go on a journey of self-discovery and self-enrichment in The Spiritual Connection. You will be guided through the meaning of spirituality, the benefits of having a relationship with God, teaching you how to recognize the signs and gifts the angels give you, showing you the benefits of raising your vibrational energy, and how we are all connected by the universal consciousness. Each one of us can make a difference in our lives, the lives of those around us and the world. We impact those around us every day; becoming aware of this, we can profoundly change all aspects of our lives and live a full, happy life.

The value of having a spiritual connection provides love, kindness, and compassion for others and yourself, you will open up to the possibilities of great transformation and potential in all areas of your life.

People are searching for purpose, for meaning in their lives, and the feeling of importance. Everyone, at some point in their life, has thought about these points and hoped for more than the 9-5 monotony they have come to know as their life. The Spiritual Connection has been written as a guide to help you live a richer, more abundant life.

As you go through each chapter, there is a section for reflecting on what you have read. There are four main areas we will look at in The Spiritual Connection.

1. What is spirituality?

2. Knowing God

3. Personal Growth

4. Full of Blessings

Part 1

What is spirituality?

Chapter 1

History of Spirituality

Understanding how spirituality has evolved throughout the centuries will help define the meaning more accurately for you. There are a variety of thoughts surrounding spirituality.

There is the belief that spirituality is in a supernatural realm. Also, more general concepts such as a quest for a sacred purpose, transcending the material aspects of life, and a sense of awe/wonderment and reverence toward the universe.

Traditionally, it has been referred to as a religious process. The term was used in early Christianity as a life oriented toward the Holy Spirit, and it expanded during the medieval times incorporating mental aspects of life.

Spirituality initially developed within early Christianity, denoting a life focused on God and Divine Spirits. The meaning broadened in the late medieval times to include mental aspects of life – "the religious scope of light versus the dark". While in modern times, the term spread to various religious traditions and expanded to refer to a broader range of experience, including a variety of esoteric traditions.

Spirituality first began to arise and entered everyday use toward the end of the Middle Ages. In the Biblical context, spirituality is to be driven or guided by the Holy Spirit.

In the 12th century, the term "spiritual," or matters concerning the spirit, is derived from Old French spiritual (originated from Latin spiritualis), which comes from spiritus or "spirit." The definition of spirit means "animating or vital principle in man and animals." Which originated from the Old French spirit, which derives from the Latin word spiritus (soul, courage, vigor, breath).

Spirituality included social and psychological meaning in the 13th century. It is socially denoting the territory of the clergy or the whole body of the clergy, regarding the nature of their office. Psychologically, the realm of the inner life: "motives, affections, intentions, inner dispositions, the psychology of spiritual life, the analysis of feelings."

There was a distinction made between higher and lower forms of spirituality in the 17th and 18th centuries. A spiritual person was more abundant and more profound than others.

The word, spirituality, was also associated with mysticism and quietism (devotional contemplation and abandonment of the will) and acquired a negative meaning. The term spirituality is now frequently used in contexts where the term "religious" once was used. Traditionally, having religious values or matters of the spirit signified being spiritual.

More recently, it has also taken on the meaning of reaching higher levels of consciousness by using meditation, yoga, and similar activities. A person becomes more attuned to everything around them, the universe, and nature.

The general meaning of spirituality is a process of re-birth which "aims to recover the original shape of man, the image of God. The spirituality of man refers to the immaterial part of his nature. The term also concerns the disposition or internal condition of a person, which prepares them to recognize and adequately appreciate spiritual realities.

In modern times, the emphasis is on the individuals personal experience. The genuine values by which people live, integrating personal growth and transformation, separate from organized religious institutions.

A variety of images have formed in the history of spirituality, which take numerous shapes and perform many functions in spirituality. Paintings and icons, sculptures and reliefs, architecture and stained glass, music, and dance, just to name a few. They played a variety of purposes: in devotional practices, meditation, healing procedures, for animation or comfort, and so forth.

True spirituality is the result of the in-working of the Holy Spirit. (1 Cor. 2:14-15) "The man without the Spirit does not accept the things that come from the Spirit of God, for they are foolishness to him, and he cannot understand them, because they are spiritually discerned.

Spirituality has become disconnected from traditional religious organizations, embracing a belief in a supernatural realm, personal growth, a quest for a holy meaning, religious experience, or an encounter with one's inner dimension or inner self.

Christian mysticism states it is the development of mystical practices and theory within Christianity and often is associated with mystical theology, especially in Catholic and Eastern Orthodox traditions. The characteristics and methods by which Christian spirituality is studied and practiced are diverse and range from the soul's spiritual relationship with God to prayerful reflection of Holy Scripture.

It was more than a century before this viewpoint evolved in the history of spirituality. Latin America, Africa, and Asia showed the socio-economic implications of forms of spirituality: women's spirituality and environmental spirituality.

Women's spirituality is directly associated with the importance of the material culture (house, clothes, food, etc.) in the spirituality of everyday life and the holiness of human life. Environmental spirituality awoke us to the earthy character of spirituality: our body, eating habits, the air we breathe, the presence of animals, the pollution of the environment, and so forth.

Hinduism identifies four ways (marga) of spiritual practice, namely Jnana, the path of knowledge. Bhakti, the path of devotion; Karma yoga, the path of selfless action; and Raja, the path of cultivating (virtues, self-discipline).

Jnana marga is a path often aided by a teacher in one's spiritual training.

Bhakti marga is a pathway of faith and dedication to a deity or divinities. The spiritual training consists of chanting, singing, and music – such as in kirtans – in front of images of one or more god or religious symbols of the divine.

Karma marga is the path of one's precise, earthly work or vartta: a job or profession that develops a spiritual practice and is achieved as a form of spiritual deliverance and not for its material rewards.

Raja marga is the path of cultivating virtues, self-discipline, tapas (meditation), contemplation, and self-reflection. Isolation and abandonment of the world, to a pinnacle state called samadhi. Reaching the state of samadhi is the peak experience.

Many people believe spirituality and religion are the same. Though all religions emphasize spirituality as part of faith, an individual can be spiritual without being religious.

Here are some of the differences between religion and spirituality.

Religion is a specific set of organized beliefs and practices, whereas spirituality is an individual's personal training focusing on a sense of peace and purpose. It also refers to the progression of developing ideas related to the meaning of life and a connection with others.

Spirituality is a way of gaining perspective on an individual's role in life and a higher meaning of their life. A spiritual person is someone whose highest priority is to be loving and caring to all around them. They believe we are all connected, a universal Oneness, and try to honor that connection. Spirituality has three aspects: relationships, values, and life purpose.

Religion focuses more on external elements: Churches or places of worship, scripture, rituals, and observances. Your attention is more on the objects in your experiences.

Spirituality focuses on your internal journey, your awareness of your soul, your inner understanding and connection with all — your higher self.

Religion is structured. Spirituality does not have a rigid structure; it is an individual's path to self-discovery.

Religion is deeply rooted in tradition, ritual, creed, and doctrine. The religious organizations guard their practices and values to preserve the teachings, so they are accurately shared through history.

Spirituality embraces change, consciousness and all who seek it – everyone. We are all part of the universe, and in such, we are all connected and welcome.

Religion is based on faith – there is an unconditional acceptance of religious teachings.

Spirituality leans more towards an individual's direct experience of your soul or divinity. The individual makes conscious contact through increased states of consciousness. In other words, you have experienced something greater through your unique universal connection rather than taking the word of another. Spirituality focuses on learning the essence of unconditional love. It is your journey of awakening.

Chapter 1 Reflection:

1. In your own words, what does spirituality mean to you?
   _____
   _____

2. What is the general concept of spirituality?
   _____
   _____

3. What is the Biblical context of spirituality?
   _____
   _____

4. How is social spirituality defined:_____
   _____
   _____

5. Psychological spirituality deal with:
   _____
   _____

6. A spiritual person is_____
   and_____ than others.

7. Spirituality is embracing:
   _____
   _____

8. What are the 4 Hinduism ways of spiritual practice?

a. _____ The path of
   _____

b. _____ The path of
   _____

c. _____ The path of
   _____

d. _____ The path of

_____

9. What is the Hinduism pinnacle state?

_____

_____

10. What are the differences between religion and spirituality?

_____

_____

_____

Chapter 2

Elements of Spirituality

Spirituality is a wide-ranging concept with room for several perspectives. Including a sense of connection to something greater than ourselves, and it typically involves a search for the purpose or meaning of the individuals' life. It is a universal human experience-something that touches us all.

The definition of spirituality is a process of personal transformation, either following religious ideals or focused on personal experience and psychological growth independent of any specific religious context. In a more general sense, it may refer to any kind of meaningful activity or blissful experience.

Knowing the techniques and beliefs of other traditions can help you gain a deeper understanding and gratitude for your spiritual journey. The core elements of all spiritual practices are Knowledge, Surrender, Meditation, Service, and Energy.

- **Knowledge** helps you gain a deeper understanding and ability to overcome obstacles. When knowledge is applied on a personal level it becomes wisdom. It is information and skills acquired through experience or education. Education cannot propel you to achieve your goals and desires, as effectively as spiritual understanding. "Fear of the Lord is the beginning of wisdom. Knowledge of the Holy One results in understanding." Proverbs 9:10

Some common benefits of knowledge are better decision-making skills, swifter problem solving, and better communication. Knowledge and wisdom help us relate to others more efficiently.

- **Surrender** is a word that brings a variety of emotions and usually is interpreted to lose or give up something. Spiritually surrendering means to give up one's own will, and subjects wholly one's thoughts, ideas, and deeds to the will and wisdom of a higher power. If you surrender to an experience or emotion, you stop trying to prevent or control it. (Cambridge dictionary)

Surrendering your control or desire over the outcome of your ideas and achievements, you will start to see the blessings God has prepared for you. It does not mean you have lost something but have given it over to One who is more knowledgeable and able to help you more effectively. You will begin to see paths unfold almost effortlessly. There will be fewer struggles, and they will be easier to maneuver.

Each one of us has experienced surrender. Picture a child trying to construct a toy, and they are getting frustrated. As a parent, we ask if they would like help and they say yes – they have surrendered control of the building process to someone more knowledgeable. We also do this as adults. Think of a time when you were getting frustrated, nothing was working, and a friend or co-worker asked if you would like help and you said yes. It is the same concept.

- **Meditation** helps calm your mind and connect to God, Angels, and the universe. You begin to deal with things in your life differently. You see life with a greater understanding and appreciation, and you start to feel universally connected. Meditation helps in reducing stress and anxiety, promotes emotional health, enhances self-awareness, lengthens your attention span, generates kindness, increases mental clarity and focus, gives you emotional intelligence, and triggers the brain's relaxation response. It can positively impact your mental and physical health.

- **Service** opens your heart to others. Helping people, even in small things, we experience great joy and love. We are here to love, support, and share with others. Most are familiar with the "Good Samaritan" parable in the Bible. (Luke 10:25-37) If not, the parable brings our attention to a stranger who has been robbed, beaten, and left on the side of the road to die. A priest and a Levite passed by, even went to the other side of the road to avoid the hurt man. Along comes a Samaritan, he saw the stranger and offered to help him. He cleaned his wounds, clothed him, and paid for him to stay at an inn nearby. His generosity went above and beyond, he asked the innkeeper to look after the man and said he would reimburse the innkeeper any extra expense that may come up.

When I was 20, I was driving to Bozeman, MT, from Billings. The trip is 140 miles, and there are several stretches where there is nothing but farmland and mountains as far as you can see. My car broke down on one of these stretches, and back then there were no cell phones and even if there were – no reception. Several cars passed by, and I was trying to figure out what I should do, as my options were: stay in the car or walk the five miles to the nearest town.

As I contemplated my next move, a truck pulled over. The most prevailing thought was I hope this person is kind and does not have ulterior motives! (My parents always told me to be cautious.) The man asked if I needed help and I explained what had happened. He offered to help me get my car to the next town. Upon arriving at the town, he looked at my car and was able to repair it enough that I could continue my journey. I am so very thankful for that Good Samaritan!

Choosing to be of service nowadays usually brings up feelings of anxiety. People think opening their heart to someone in need could be dangerous, or those in need will not use the generosity the way you intended they should. Remember, it is not our place to decide how they use our gift to them – only that we give it.

You receive blessings for following your heart and showing love and kindness. Do not hold back your generosity because of another's free will. I have always tried to instill this advice – following your inner voice which shows you how you can help someone is beautiful.

There are many ways we can be of service to others. Create lunch bags filled with the cheese and cracker snacks, perhaps a protein bar and a bottle of water. When you come across someone alongside the road or on a street corner holding up a sign asking for help – give them one of the bags. Tutor students, mentor, help a neighbor with yard work, volunteer, send someone a card letting them know they are in your thoughts. It is as simple as reaching out to someone. The possibilities are endless!

- **Energy** is all around us. Everything is energy, our thoughts, and dreams, plants, air, earth. Learning to feel the energy that is all around will help you discern events and situations in a more uplifting way. Have you ever noticed walking into a room and feeling the excitement in the air, or someone comes up to you that is struggling, and you begin to feel tired?

The world around us is full of energy. We are energy, every cell in our body. Learning to discern the negative and positive energies will help each one of us live better. Negative energy drains positive energy, and likewise, positive energy eliminates negative energy.

Spirituality relates more to your search and personal growth, to finding greater meaning and purpose in your life-your Divine destiny. Spirituality links you with the powerful and divine forces that are present in the universe. Spiritual awareness and unique spiritual experience are sacred — a deep sense of exhilaration and connection through the universal consciousness.

Spirituality is the foundation of divinity that pulsates, dances, and flows as the source and essence of every soul. It relates more to your search, to find greater meaning and purpose in your existence.

We all have a unique connection with our surroundings, nature, and people. For example: Have you ever thought of a friend whom you have not spoken to for a while, and they call? How about knowing there is a storm coming even though the forecast is clear, and it comes? Or knowing a natural disaster is about to happen, i.e., earthquake, tornado, etc.

When we attune our inner voice, and trust our intuition, we become more centered; our focus is more direct. Instead of feeling like you are on an inner tube drifting aimlessly out of control on the river of life, you begin to take charge. You no longer second guess yourself, and you will gain clarity.

Elements of Spirituality include (but are not limited to):

- Look beyond outer appearances to the more profound significance and soul of everything
- Love and respect for Divine Powers
- Love and respect for yourself
- Love and respect for all things

Spirituality is not defined by religion, but by the individual. Spirituality is not the same as religion, though many times, people associate them with each other. Religion is an organized group or culture that has been sparked by a spiritual or divine soul. They act through a mission and intention of presenting specific teachings and doctrines while nurturing and generating a particular way of life.

Spirituality is:

- Beyond all religions yet encompassing all religions
- Beyond all science still including all science
- Beyond all philosophy yet encompassing all philosophy.

As one becomes more spiritual, animalistic aggressions of fighting and trying to manipulate or control others will be cast off.

Each step down the path and even the pathway itself – is a personal connection to God, Source, Spirit, and to the universe that can be as unique as the individual making the journey.

Traditionally, being spiritual implied having an attachment to religious values or matters of the spirit, rather than material or worldly interests. More recently, it has changed to mean reaching advanced levels of awareness through meditation, yoga, and similar practices.

Spirituality is a state in which we connect to Divine Powers, Nature, each other, and the deepest part of ourselves.

The whole struggle on the planet is not between good and evil. It has always been one man's belief versus another's. The need for understanding is more psychological than spiritual. You want to cling to something, you want to feel secure, you want to feel like you know all. The problem is if you do not know anything about this way of life, you are not able to access your full potential spiritually. You learn about this existence by tapping into something greater than yourself – universal knowledge; with that, you see how to change yourself into a joyful, healthy, and vibrant person, which is within your hands.

Healthy spirituality gives a sense of peace, wholeness, and balance among the physical, emotional, social, and spiritual aspects of our lives. However, the path to such spirituality passes through struggles and suffering and often includes experiences that are frightening and painful.

Modern spirituality theorists claim that spirituality builds inner peace and forms a foundation for happiness. For example, meditation and similar practices are recommended to help practitioners cultivate their inner life and character. Spirituality causes a wide array of favorable health effects, as well as morale, happiness, and life fulfillment.

Opening your mind and heart to the benefits of spirituality will ultimately help guide you on your life journey more prepared and give you comfort.

Chapter 2 Reflection:

1. What is the definition of spirituality?

   _____

   _____

   _____

2. What is your experience with spirituality?

   _____

   _____

   _____

   _____

3. What are the core elements of all spiritual practices? Explain what each one means to you.

   a. _____

      _____

   b. _____

      _____

   c. _____

      _____

   d. _____

      _____

4. What are the benefits of knowledge?

   a. _____

   b. _____

   c. _____

5. What does it mean to spiritually surrender?

_____

_____

_____

6. What are the benefits of meditation? _____

_____

_____

_____

7. Is there a service you have always wanted to do to help others?

_____

    If so, what? _____

8. Have you ever thought about the energy you have?

_____

_____

9. What does spirituality link you to?

_____

_____

10. Spirituality is the foundation of:

_____

_____

11. What are the elements of spirituality?

_____

_____

_____

12. What is religion? _____

_____

_____

_____

13. Spirituality is:

_____

_____

_____

_____

14. What does healthy spirituality give you?

_____

_____

_____

Chapter 3

Importance of Spirituality

Our mind, body, and soul must be in harmony with each other to function adequately; therefore, we must be balanced. If we are out of balance, we will feel overwhelmed by our emotions – overly sensitive, fearful, or have a feeling of being out of control. We react to situations instead of responding to them. One way we can tell if we are not allowing ourselves to handle the moment with our intuition is how we feel afterward. Feeling remorse or guilt lets us know we did not handle the situation in the best way possible.

On the other hand, if we feel like we have handled the situation with dignity and respect, we have responded intuitively and genuinely feel good. As we become balanced, we will be able to cope easily with emotions that arise. That is not to say it will not affect us, but it will be easier to deal with. We will no longer look at the past or toward the future with negative emotions or fear attached. Feeling emotionally and spiritually balanced, we begin to feel more centered and connected to others, the universe, and our inner self. Thus, feeling connected, we become in tune with our subconscious, our Divine Spirit (whether that is God, Buddha, or other Divine Spirit), nature, and others.

We experience spiritual moments when we walk through the woods and connect with nature, walk along a beautiful beach or when we see the sunset or sunrise, or simply listening to inspirational music. We are then genuinely in tune with Divine Powers, nature, each other, and ourselves.

Our intuition or inner voice helps guide us in our life's purpose. We begin to look at our surroundings and strive to become better intuitively. We have a calmness, a peace that can only be attained by tuning into our subconscious. The Oxford dictionary describes intuition as the ability to understand something immediately, without the need for conscious reasoning.

Meditation is a wonderful way to begin listening to our inner voice and bringing balance to our lives.

Chapter 3 Reflection:

1. Do you listen to your intuition? If so, give an
    example of when.

    _____

    _____

    _____

    _____

2. Do you feel connected? If so, explain how it feels to
    you.

    _____

    _____

    _____

    _____

3. Name three spiritual moments you have
    experienced.

    a. _____

    b. _____

    c. _____

4. When we are balanced, we begin to feel
    _____ & _____.

5. What does our inner voice (intuition) help with?

    _____

    _____

    _____

    _____

Chapter 4

Spiritual Journey

Spirituality is a lifelong process. Life will hit us with tragedy or good fortune, and our level of spirituality will determine how well we handle it. We have two options in dealing with life events. One, we hide away from the world, letting depression and anxiety take over; or two, we can take the experience and learn from it.

I have had a couple of life-altering events that have shaken me to my core. The choices I made would impact my entire family for the rest of their lives. You see, when tragedy hits, it usually does not just hit you but everyone around you. You may be affected the most, and your actions will determine how much others are affected. I chose to face those situations head-on and help those around me – even though I was heartbroken.

My world shattered the day I received a call informing me my 24-year-old daughter died; we had no warning. A few moments before I got the call, her father asked me if I had heard from her. She was going to Alaska to visit her dad. My daughter and I had not talked in a couple of days, so I tried calling her to see if she made it to the airport, of course, she did not answer. She had planned to have a friend pick her up and take her to the airport. Her friend got to her apartment and tried contacting her for almost 30 minutes, when she did not respond, he woke up her roommates. They went to wake her up, but she was already gone.

After the coroner called, I had to call her father and tell him. I vividly remember him saying, "NO, No, No, it can't be, No!" Next, I tried to contact my other daughter. My heart broke with every phone call I made that day. Hearing the grief and sadness on the other end of the phone only compounded my sorrow. Shortly after calling my husband, my sister-in-law got to our house. She watched my son while I went to my daughters' house to tell her what happened.

Again, vividly, I recall her response, she ran into her bedroom, collapsed, screaming, "No, No, No!" The moment I got the call my world stopped, I was going through the motions of what was needed, but I recall deep despair and anguish.

My choices in dealing with this tragedy: hide from everything, immersed in the pain and sorrow, or face my pain. Dealing with it as it came – usually in tsunami waves from day to day – and help my family and all my daughters' amazing friends deal with the loss. I chose to honor my daughter's memory and celebrate the short life she had and be there for all those she loved. We traveled to California and spent a week with her friends, crying, laughing, and sharing beautiful memories. Doing this is not always easy, and sadness can be overwhelming, but I have found great comfort in helping others. My family takes a yearly trip to visit her friends; and, to me, they have become an extension of our family.

I began a quest to help ease the grief and become more in tune with my inner self.

Below are the steps I have taken to tap into healing and gain a fuller life experience.

1. Take time for yourself daily.

Rejuvenate your spirit and nurture yourself by listening to relaxing music. Read an inspirational book, meditate, or take a walk. This is extremely helpful in strengthening your spirit and giving you the ability to face each day with wisdom and understanding.

2. Look around your neighborhood or community and volunteer, help those in need.

You automatically connect better with humanity when you help others. This changes your focus from self and allows for healing to take place. Remember: that which we do for ourselves we take to our grave; that which we do for others will live on for eternity. Helping others allows you to rejoice in the bigger picture and help you keep your heart open and aware of others.

3. Practice gratitude.

This can be a challenge when you are grieving, but it also helps you see blessings, and keep your heart open to those around you. A person who looks at life with a grateful heart finds happiness in the smallest areas. They are the people that light up a room with positive energy, love, and joy. Look around you, be thankful for what you see, your friends, family, pets, home, vehicle, job, etc.

4. Practice Mindfulness.

Become aware of your environment and yourself within your environment. Mindfulness is maintaining a moment-by-moment awareness of everything around us, our environment, our thoughts, and our feelings. You begin to trust your intuition as your awareness increases.

5. Express yourself.

Become involved in creative or expressive activities, learn to dance, sing, play a musical instrument, write, or paint. Creative activities allow you to express the emotions you are dealing with positively and put them into something beautiful. This helps you process the emotion you cannot put into words.

One of the most significant gifts of spiritual knowledge is it restores your sense of self to something you may not have ever imagined within you. Spirituality says that even if you think you are limited and small, it simply is not true. A great and divine light exists within you.

You feel great inspiration when filled with spiritual energy. You begin to see opportunities that you may have overlooked in the past.

On your spiritual journey, there are two main themes you will experience:

- Allowing overwhelming inspiration, which also translates into love, joy and wisdom, peacefulness, and service.
- Realizing an inevitable expiration or death awaits to take you away from the very circumstances you feel are important right now.

Chapter 4 Reflection:

1. What are the two options in dealing with life events?

   a. _____

   b. _____

2. What are the 5 steps for connecting with your inner self?

   a. _____

   b. _____

   c. _____

   d. _____

   e. _____

3. Do you take time daily for yourself?

   _____

   _____

   If so, what do you do? _____

   If not, what is holding you back?

   _____

4. What are some ways you could or do help others?

   _____

   _____

   _____

5. List some things you are grateful to have in your life.

   a. _____

b. _____

c. _____

d. _____

e. _____

6. How do you practice mindfulness?

_____

_____

_____

7. What creative activities do you enjoy?

_____

_____

_____

8. How often do you take the time to do them?

_____

_____

_____

Part 2

Knowing God

Chapter 5

God/Holy Spirit

Realize, God wants a close, personal relationship with you. All that is needed from you is to seek it, set time aside daily for Him. You would do that for a friend, why not for God?

First, let us take a moment to see who God is and how He wants to be involved with each one of us. Remember: God is always working around you and your life. He wants you to learn to hear His voice and know His will. The goal of God's activity in your life is that you come to KNOW Him.

Who is God? What is the Holy Spirit?

These are age-old questions that are extremely important. Understanding, who God is, we must look at His character and attributes, what He is like, in essence. The all-encompassing Spiritual Being as explained in the Bible.

As I grew up, I was introduced to Church a little bit. I have fond memories of Sunday School – nothing more. Sunday School taught me "Jesus" loved me. He watched over me and thought I was special. I wanted to go back every week to hear more about "Jesus," and yes, how special He thought I was.

I still love Sunday School, but seldom does it mention how much Jesus loves you or how special He thinks each one of us is to Him. The sermons, preaching, and teachings are about affliction, sin, and condemnation. Why is that?

Being older does not mean we do not want or need to hear about His love for us or that He thinks we are unique.

Most people spend their entire life seeking love, acceptance, and to feel special. They are searching for the person who will complete them when what they need is a direction. There will continuously be a void in your heart if your search is limited to a person. Please do not misunderstand. You can and will find love – God has someone specific for each one of us, but your search should be inward to fill the void. Once you are content with who you are or who you are becoming, then you will find that special someone who inexplicably compliments your being. First, you must learn to love yourself. You are unique. You are precious. Yes, you can and will find a special someone along your journey, but they will not compliment you as well and perhaps even hinder your journey. I am not saying do not look until you are content with yourself, just be cautious as to who you allow to join you on your path.

We are as children taking that first step toward Mommy or Daddy, unsure, perhaps scared- reaching out for the arms that comfort; this is how we are to be towards God. He wants to comfort us, to cheer us on, to help us if, and when, we fall.

The difference between us as a child and us as an adult is that a child will get back up because their goal is to be in Mommy or Daddy's arms. As adults, when we fall, we decide that if we get up, we will get hurt again, so it is best to stay where we are. Why? We do not like pain and the feeling of failure. Perhaps we are even demanding that God or the Divine Powers come to us.

Look at Matthew 18:3, "And he said; I tell you the truth unless you change and become like little children, you will never enter the kingdom of heaven."

A child never gives up until they reach their goal, what they want, what they have their eye on. We are no different than that child, we have just given up, decided it is too much effort and we would only get hurt. We are all children. Some of us listen, some obey, and some rebel. The choice is always ours.

Seeking spirituality first is essential. Everything else in life will become perfectly arranged.

We rush through our lives, only realizing, in the end, we did not have a chance to live. We hurry through life, not recognizing what we are missing.

Remember! Every obstacle we come up against:

- God has a blueprint, and we are part of that plan.
- God can overcome EVERYTHING!

In the Christian faith, accepting and asking God into your life endows you with every attribute and characteristic of God. This enabling and perfecting power of grace is available through the principles of faith, repentance, humility, diligence, obedience, and seeking the Spirit and its gifts. Faith is sufficient to change you, transform you, and perfect you; to enable you to realize your vast potential as a child of God fully.

The root of the word "divine" is literally "godly" (from the Latin deus, cf Dyaus, closely related to Greek Zeus, div in Persian and deva in Sanskrit), but the use varies significantly depending on which deity is studied.

Knowing God's mercy helps us understand how some principles fully enable grace to fill us. Faith in Jesus Christ is the first principle that welcomes God's grace. (Romans 5:1-2 "Therefore, since we have been justified through faith, we have peace with God through our Lord Jesus Christ, through whom we have gained access by faith into this grace in which we now stand. And we rejoice in the hope of the glory of God."). Truth, hope, action, and confirming witness are the essential elements of faith and are the pathway to receiving the Lord's grace.

Peter relates how "God anointed Jesus of Nazareth with the Holy Spirit and with power, went about doing good and healing all who were oppressed by the devil, for

God was with Him" (Acts 10:38). The Holy Spirit, the power by which God was with Him-the power which Jesus Christ was able to perform great miracles during His ministry on Earth. The Holy Spirit is the presence of God's power actively working in His servants.

This statement is important! Repeat this statement, only this time change His servants to you or put your name in its place:

The Holy Spirit is the presence of God's power actively working in you.

Let us look at who God is in the Bible.

The Trinity: God, Jesus, and the Holy Spirit

The concept of the Trinity can be overwhelming. In 1 John 5:7-8, "For there are three that bear record in heaven, the Father, the Word, and the Holy Ghost; and these three are one. And there are three that bear witness in earth, the Spirit and the water, and the blood, and these three agree in one." The meaning to bear witness is to show something exists or is true.

2 Corinthians 13:14, "May the grace of the Lord Jesus Christ, and the love of God, and the fellowship of the Holy Spirit be with you all." This verse tells us we can have the grace and love of God with us, and He wants fellowship – a relationship, and companionship with us.

These verses reference three separate entities yet also say they are one. How can this be? Let us look at this question from a different viewpoint, water. Water can be liquid, ice, and steam, but all are water in various forms. In this viewpoint, God is the liquid, Jesus is the ice, and the Holy Spirit is the steam; all are the same, water – just in different forms. A beautiful way to explain the Trinity.

God, our Creator

Genesis 1:1 "In the beginning, God created the heavens and the earth."

The miracle of creation found in Genesis 1-2 goes through every step God took in the creation process.

Psalm 146:5-6 "Happy is he that hath the God of Jacob for his help, whose hope is in the Lord his God; which made heaven, and earth, the sea and all that therein is; which keepeth truth for ever."

Colossians 1:16 "For by him were all things created, that are in heaven, and that are in earth, visible and invisible, whether they be thrones, or dominions, or principalities, or powers; all things were created by Him and for Him." In the chapter on Angels, the thrones, dominions, principalities, and powers will be explained.

John 1:3 "Through Him, all things were made; without him, nothing was made that has been made."

God, our Advocate

An advocate is someone who publicly supports an individual, cause, or policy. The role of an advocate seeks to ensure that people are heard regarding issues that are important to them, to safeguard and defend them. They plead for a person's cause on their behalf.

Romans 8:25-26 "But if we hope for what we do not yet have, we wait for it patiently. In the same way, the Spirit helps us in our weakness. We do not know what we ought to pray for, but the Spirit himself intercedes for us with groans that words cannot express." Intercede is to speak on an individual's behalf. What a beautiful verse! Most of the time, I am not sure what I should pray – Thank God! He took that into account!

Romans 8:34 "Who is he that condemns? Christ Jesus, who died – more than that, who was raised to life – is at the right hand of God and is also interceding for us."

Jesus speaks on our behalf, even if we do not have the words or know what we need. We have an excellent companion that stands up for us and fights for us.

Chapter 5 Reflection:

1. What does God want from us?

   _____

   _____

2. Who is God to you?

   _____

   _____

   _____

   _____

3. What is the Holy Spirit to you?

   _____

   _____

   _____

   _____

4. Every obstacle:

   a. _____

   b. _____

5. Faith is sufficient to:

   a. _____

   b. _____

   c. _____

   d. _____

6. What are the essential elements of faith?

   a. _____

   b. _____

   c. _____

   d. _____

7. In your own words describe who the Holy Spirit is:

_____

_____

_____

8. What is the Trinity?_____

_____

_____

_____

9. What is an advocate?_____

_____

_____

_____

10. What does having an advocate mean to you?

_____

_____

_____

11. What are the two choices we have in facing every obstacle?

  a. _____
  b. _____

Chapter 6

God's Attributes

Attributes are qualities or features regarded as an inherent part of an individual. They are the unchanging qualities that makeup who you are.

God is Omnipotent, having unlimited power.

Omnipotent comes from the Latin words (Omn or omnes), meaning all and (potens) meaning power.

Psalm 93:4 "Mightier than the thunder of the great waters, mightier than the breakers of the sea – the Lord on high is mighty."

Jeremiah 32:17 "Ah, Sovereign Lord, you have made the heavens and the earth by your great power and outstretched arm. Nothing is too hard for you."

Matthew 19:26 "Jesus looked at them and said, with man this is impossible, but with God, all things are possible."

God has our backs; nothing is impossible with a friend like Him on our side.

God is Omniscient, all-knowing.

The meaning of Omniscient is to have infinite awareness, understanding, and insight. There is nothing God is not aware of, past, present, and future.

Psalm 139:1-6 "O Lord, you have searched me, and you know me. You know when I sit and when I rise; you perceive my thoughts from afar. You discern my going out and my lying down; you are familiar with all my ways. Before a word is on my tongue, you know it completely, O Lord. You hem me in – behind and before; you have laid your hand upon me. Such knowledge is too wonderful for me, too lofty for me to attain."

Proverbs 5:21 "For a man's ways are in full view of the Lord, and he examines all his paths."

He knows which path is the best for us if we listen. He will guide us.

God is Omnipresent.

God is present everywhere at the same time. His divine presence encompasses the entire universe. He is not bound by space or time.

Psalm 46:1 "God is our refuge and strength, an ever-present help in trouble."

Psalm 139:7-10 "Where can I go from your Spirit? Where can I flee from your presence? If I go up to the heavens, you are there; if I make my bed in the depths, you are there. If I rise on the wings of the dawn, if I settle on the far side of the sea, even there your hand will guide me, your right hand will hold me fast."

He is always near us; all we must do is ask for Him to join us in our day. If we do not ask-He will still be there, but He will be watching us from the sidelines-we will not receive the guidance and love as effectively.

God is Eternal.

Eternal is lasting or existing forever – no beginning and no end and is related to the state of being timeless. He has no beginning and no end.

Psalm 90:1-2 "Lord, you have been our dwelling place throughout all generations. Before the mountains were born or you brought forth the earth and the world, from everlasting to everlasting, you are God."

Lamentations 5:19 "You, O Lord, reign forever; your throne endures from generation to generation."

Many people get stuck on this concept because our thinking is finite-limited. Everything we know has a beginning and an end from our bodies to plants, even the vehicles we drive. Let us look at this from the viewpoint of the universe itself. Space has always existed; it will still exist when everything else disappears. We have nothing that proves without a shadow of a doubt that the universe did not exist at one point. There are theories but nothing else.

The definition of the universe is all existing matter and space considered as a whole, the cosmos. It is believed to be at 10 billion light-years in diameter and contains a vast number of galaxies, with the Big Bang Theory it has changed to 13.8 billion light-years. The universe is everything we can touch, feel, sense, measure and detect. It includes living things, planets, stars, galaxies, dust clouds, light, and time. The universe encompasses everything in existence, from the smallest atom to the largest galaxy.

God is greater than the universe; He created everything. He is eternal and infinite.

God is Infinite.

His power and knowledge exist in unlimited abundance. Infinity is anything that cannot be counted or measured, many dimensions. The definition of infinite is limitless or endless space, extent, or size; impossible to measure or calculate. Something that never ends.

Isaiah 40:28 "Do you not know? Have you not heard? The Lord is the everlasting God, the Creator of the ends of the earth. He will not grow tired or weary, and his understanding no one can fathom."

1 Kings 8:27 "But will God really dwell on the earth? The heavens, even the highest heaven, cannot contain you. How much less this temple I have built."

God is Immutable.

He does not change; He is consistent. No matter what is going on, He is always the same. God is unchanging in His character, will, and promises.

Malachi 3:6, "I the Lord do not change. So, you, O descendants of Jacob, are not destroyed."

Hebrews 1:10-12 "In the beginning, O Lord, you laid the foundations of the earth, and the heavens are the work of your hands. They will perish, but you remain; they will all wear out like a garment. You will roll them up like a robe; like a garment, they will be changed. But you remain the same, and your years will never end."

Hebrews 13:8 "Jesus Christ is the same yesterday and today and forever."

James 1:17 "Every good and perfect gift is from above, coming down from the Father of the heavenly lights, who does not change like shifting shadows."

God is Incomprehensible.

The Cambridge dictionary meaning incomprehensible is impossible or extremely difficult to understand. We can also use the word unfathomable or incapable of being measured.

Ecclesiastes 11:5 "As you do not know the path of the wind, or how the body is formed in a mother's womb, so you cannot understand the work of God, the Maker of all things."

Isaiah 55:8-9 "For my thoughts are not your thoughts, neither are your way my ways, declares the Lord, as the heavens are higher than the earth, so are my ways higher than your ways and my thoughts than your thoughts."

Isaiah 40:28 "Do you not know? Have you not heard? The Lord is the everlasting God, the Creator of the ends of the earth. He will not grow tired or weary, and his understanding no one can fathom."

Now, let us look at the Periodic Table. Most of us are familiar with this from school. We cannot see the atoms and electrons without a microscope, and most of us do not have one handy to use daily. We are trusting the information we learned about the elements in the periodic table to be accurate and correct. Just because we cannot see something with our eyes does not mean it does not exist.

The element recipe of water is two parts hydrogen and 1-part oxygen. We cannot see hydrogen or oxygen, but we have evidence they exist when they are combined to form H_2O-water. When we begin to expand our consciousness, our awareness of the world around us heightens. We begin to feel things and see things differently. We start to connect with the universe and God and gain clarity. We will no longer feel alone; instead, we will feel divinely connected to everything.

We cannot see God with our eyes. But looking at how intricate our bodies are, the way everything works together from photosynthesis to each cell – none of this is possible from an origin of chaos as chaos creates more chaos, we can conclude He exists. There is decisiveness in the creation of all things in our universe. Systems work intricately and precisely with each other. This was not by accident but thoroughly thought out. Here are a couple items to ponder.

Similar to the water element recipe, the human element recipe is: 1 part Holy Spirit (spark of light from God that guides us and helps us discern right from wrong), 1 part Soul (our inner being, that which is greater than our physical body; our gut feelings, senses), 3 parts Love (compassion) and 1 part Physical Matter (our physical body).

Chapter 6 Reflection:

1. What are attributes?_____

   _____

   _____

   _____

2. What does each attribute mean to you?

   a. Omnipotent:

   _____

   _____

   b. Omniscient:

   _____

   _____

   c. Omnipresent:

   _____

   _____

   d. Eternal:

   _____

   _____

   e. Infinite:

   _____

   _____

   f. Immutable:

   _____

   _____

   g. Incomprehensible:

   _____

   _____

3. How do you feel knowing you have a friend like God with you?

_____

_____

_____

4. What are your attributes?_____

_____

_____

_____

Chapter 7

The Character of God

Character is mental and moral qualities distinctive to an individual. The way someone thinks feels and behaves, their personality.

The Sovereignty of God.

The supreme power or authority. God is the supreme authority, and all things are under His control.

Job 42:2 "I know that you can do all things; no plan of yours can be thwarted."

Psalm 33:11 "But the plans of the Lord stand firm forever, the purposes of his heart through all generations."

Isaiah 46:10, "I make known the end from the beginning, from ancient times, what is still to come. I say, my purpose will stand, and I will do all that I please."

The Holiness of God.

He is both exalted and worthy of complete devotion and morally pure.

Matthew 5:48, "Be perfect; therefore, as your heavenly Father is perfect."

Exodus 15:11 "Who among the gods is like you, O Lord? Who is like you – majestic in holiness, awesome in glory, working wonders?"

Isaiah 6:3, "And they were calling to one another: "Holy, Holy, Holy is the Lord Almighty; the whole earth is full of His glory."

Revelations 4:8 "Each of the four living creatures had six wings and was covered with eyes all around, even under his wings. Day and night, they never stop saying: Holy, Holy, Holy is the Lord God Almighty, who was, and is, and is to come."

The Righteousness of God.

Righteousness is the quality of being morally right. Being righteous is acting in accord with divine or moral law: free from guilt or sin. (Merriam-Webster definition)

Romans 1:17 "For in the gospel, a righteousness from God is revealed, a righteousness that is by faith from the first to last, just as it is written: the righteous will live by faith."

Psalm 11:7 "For the Lord is righteous; he loves justice; upright men will see his face."

Psalm 33:4-5 "For the Work of the Lord is right and true; he is faithful in all he does."

Psalm 145:17, "The Lord is righteous in all his ways and loving toward all he has made."

The Greatness of God.

Greatness is excellence that emanates from the inside out, impacting those around you out of passion, love, kindness, and inspiration.

Deuteronomy 3:24 "O Sovereign Lord, you have begun to show to your servant your greatness and your strong hand. For what god is there in heaven or on earth who can do the deeds and mighty works you do?"

Job 37:5 "God's voice thunders in marvelous ways; he does great things beyond our understanding."

Psalm 104:1, "Praise the Lord, O my soul. O Lord my God, you are very great; you are clothed with splendor and majesty."

The Wisdom of God.

God always wills the highest purposes and proper means to achieve those purposes for His glory and His peoples' blessing.

Psalm 25:8-9 "The Lord is good and does what is right; he shows the proper path to those who go astray. He leads the humble in what is right, teaching them his way."

Romans 11:33 "Oh, the depth of the riches of the wisdom and knowledge of God! How unsearchable his judgments, and his paths beyond tracing out."

Psalm 104:24, "How many are your works, O Lord! In wisdom you made them all; the earth is full of your creatures."

The Love of God.

God always gives of Himself. The definition of love in the Bible takes us to 1 Corinthians 13:4-7 "Love is patient, love is kind. It does not envy; it does not boast; it is not proud. It is not rude; it is not self-seeking; it is not easily angered; it keeps no record of wrongs. Love does not delight in evil but rejoices with the truth. It always protects, always trusts, always hopes, always perseveres."

John 3:16 "God so loved the world that he gave his only son so that everyone who believes in him will not perish but have eternal life."

1 John 4:7-9 "Dear friends, let us love one another, for love comes from God. Everyone who loves has been born of God and knows God. Whoever does not love does not know God, because God is love. This is how God showed his love among us: He sent his one and only Son into the world that we might live through him."

Jeremiah 31:3 "The Lord appeared to us in the past, saying: I have loved you with an everlasting love; I have drawn you with loving-kindness."

1 John 3:1 "See how very much our heavenly Father loves us, for he allows us to be called his children, and we really are! But the people who belong to this world do not know God, so they don't understand that we are his children."

1 John 3:18 "Dear children, let us not love with words or tongue but with actions and in truth."

Romans 5:5 "We know how dearly God loves us because he has given us the Holy Spirit to fill our hearts with his love."

The Faithfulness of God.

He brings all His power, love, compassion, and dedication to you — the unwavering loyalty to a person or the oath or promise.

Isaiah 25:1 "O Lord, you are my God, I will exalt you and praise your name, for in perfect faithfulness you have done marvelous things, things planned long ago."

2 Timothy 2:13, "If we are faithless, he will remain faithful, for he cannot disown himself."

Hebrews 10:23 "Let us hold unswervingly to the hope we profess, for he who promised is faithful."

The Mercy of God.

Mercy is compassion, forgiveness, and kindness for all of us. Mercy is showing someone compassion and forgiveness, even though they have betrayed or hurt us. As humans, we have a difficult time showing mercy to others. They have wronged us and therefore should be punished, period. Thank God He does not think that way! We think in finite terms where God looks towards the goal: having a relationship with us.

Look at this through the eyes of a parent. Our children make mistakes, hurt us and usually, as teenagers, they will disobey us and perhaps even betray us. Does that mean we no longer love them? Of course not. We show mercy on them because we want them in our lives. That does not mean they will not be punished, but we will not withhold our love. Our goal is to have a relationship with them. Remember: We are God's children. He loves us and wants to have a relationship with us.

Lamentations 3:22-23 "Because of the Lord's great love we are not consumed, for his compassions never fail. They are new every morning; great is your faithfulness."

Ephesians 2:4-5 "But because of his great love for us, God, who is rich in mercy, made us alive with Christ even when we were dead in transgressions – it is by grace you have been saved."

Psalm 103:8 "The Lord is merciful and gracious; he is slow to get angry and full of unfailing love."

The Forgiveness of God.

Forgiveness is a conscious, intentional choice to release feelings of resentment or vengeance toward a person or group who has harmed you, regardless of whether they deserve it or not.

Mark 11:25 "And when you stand praying, if you hold anything against anyone, forgive him, so that your Father in heaven may forgive you your sins."

Micah 7:18-19 "Who is a God like you, who pardons sin and forgives the transgression of the remnant of his inheritance? You do not stay angry forever but delight to show mercy."

The Graciousness of God.

Graciousness inspires noble aspirations and imparts strength to endure trials and resist temptations and as an individual virtue or excellence of divine origin.

Psalm 116:5, "The Lord is gracious and righteous; our God is full of compassion."

Isaiah 30:18 "Yet the Lord longs to be gracious to you; he rises to show you compassion. For the Lord is a God of justice. Blessed are all who wait for Him!"

Ephesians 2:6-7 "And God raised us up with Christ and seated us with him in the heavenly realms in Christ Jesus, in order that in the coming ages he might show the incomparable riches of his grace, expressed in his kindness to us in Christ Jesus."

Exodus 34:5-6 "Then the Lord came down in the cloud and stood there with him and proclaimed his name, the Lord. And he passed in front of Moses, proclaiming, "The Lord, the Lord, the compassionate and gracious God, slow to anger, abounding in love and faithfulness."

1 Peter 2:2-3 "Like newborn babies, crave pure spiritual milk, so that by it you may grow up in your salvation, now that you have tasted that the Lord is good."

The Truthfulness of God

He always tells the truth and always fulfills His promises. He is sincere. The Biblical meaning of truthfulness is that which is consistent with the mind, will, character, glory, and being of God. Truth cannot contradict itself.

Numbers 23:19 "God is not a man, that He should lie, nor a son of man, that he should change His mind. Does He speak and then not act? Does he promise and not fulfill?"

The Longsuffering of God

The definition of longsuffering is having or showing patience despite troubles, especially those caused by other people, patiently enduring lasting offense, or hardship.

He waits for us as a parent waits for their children.

Psalm 103:8 "The Lord is compassionate and gracious, slow to anger, abounding in love."

Romans 2:4 "Or do you show contempt of the riches of kindness, tolerance, and patience, not realizing that God's kindness leads you towards repentance."

2 Peter 3:9 "The Lord is not slow in keeping His promise, as some understand slowness. He is patient with you, not wanting anyone to perish, but everyone to come to repentance."

The Goodness of God

Goodness is the quality of being morally good or virtuous. It is integrity, honesty, and upright – having high moral standards in all areas of life.

Psalm 31:19, "How great is your goodness, which you have stored up for those who fear you, which you bestow in the sight of men on those who take refuge in you."

Nahum 1:7 "The Lord is good, a refuge in times of trouble."

The Justice of God

Justice means to be morally fair, to make right.

Deuteronomy 32:4 "He is a Rock, His works are perfect, and all His ways are just."

Isaiah 30:18 "Yet the Lord longs to be gracious to you; He rises to show you compassion. For the Lord is a God of Justice. Blessed are all who wait for Him!"

Romans 3:26 "He did it to demonstrate His justice at the present time, so as to be just and the one who justifies those who have faith in Jesus."

The Wrath of God

Wrath is extreme anger, punishment for an offense or crime.

Jeremiah 10:10 "But the Lord is the true God; He is the Living God, the eternal King. When He is angry, the earth trembles; the nations cannot endure His wrath."

Romans 5:8-9 "But God demonstrates His own love for us in this: While we were still sinners, Christ died for us. Since we have now been justified by his blood, how much more shall we be saved from God's wrath through him!"

Exodus 15:7 "In the greatness of your majesty, you threw down those who opposed you. You unleashed your burning anger; it consumed them like stubble."

Psalm 69:24 "Pour out your wrath on them; let your fierce anger overtake them."

John 3:36 "Whoever believes in the Son has eternal life, but whoever rejects the Son will not see life, for God's wrath remains on him."

The Jealousy of God

God desires to protect the love relationship we have with Him or to avenge it when that relationship has been broken.

Exodus 34:14 "Do not worship any other god, for the Lord, whose name is Jealous, is a jealous God."

Deuteronomy 4:24 "For the Lord, your God is a consuming fire, a jealous God."

Nahum 1:2 "The Lord is a jealous and avenging God; the Lord takes vengeance and is filled with wrath. The Lord takes vengeance on his foes and maintains his wrath against his enemies."

Exodus 20:4-6 "You shall not make for yourself an idol in the form of anything in heaven above or on the earth beneath or in the waters below. You shall not bow down to them or worship them; for I, the Lord your God, am a jealous God, punishing the children for the sin of the fathers to the third and fourth generation of those who hate me, but showing love to a thousand generations of those who love me and keep my commandments."

Chapter 7 Reflection:

1. What are God's characteristics? What do they mean to you?

   _____

   _____

   _____

   _____

2. What does the Bible say about love? (1 Corinthians 13:4-7)

Love is   Love is not

_____   _____

_____   _____

_____   _____

Love does   Love does not

_____   _____

_____   _____

Love always

_____

_____

Chapter 8

God Sent Angels

The definition of an angel is a messenger. Angels are all around us every moment. They try to communicate with us in a variety of ways. Unfortunately, most do not know what to look for or are so busy they do not pay attention. The angels are here to help us, guide us, warn us, comfort us, and protect us. They watched over us when times are good and when times are tough. Their wings wrap gently around us and are continually whispering in our ear – "you are loved."

The intention of Angels:

1. Protect us against narrow thinking toward all the creations of God.
2. Help us in developing a proper understanding of Christ.
3. Help us comprehend the unseen world to which we are hastening.
4. Give us an example of joyous and perfect fulfillment of God's will. Matthew 6:10, "Your

kingdom come, Your will be done on earth as it is in heaven."

5. Help us see the great joy of salvation in heaven. "There is joy in the presence of the angels of God over one sinner who repents" (Luke 15:10).

6. Expand our view of the mercies of God and remind us we are special to God, whose angels are "sent out to render service for the sake of those who will inherit salvation" (Hebrews 1:14)

7. Remind us of our importance to God as human beings and our glorious destiny as Christians. "You made him a little lower than the heavenly beings and crowned him with glory and honor" (Psalm 8:5), "May become like angels in heaven" (Matthew 22:30).

Angels send us gifts to let us know they are with us. Some examples are feathers in our path, finding coins, hearing a song on the radio. You may feel comforted, feel a tingle in your hair, or someone is touching your arm. You will see bright sparkles at the corner of your eyes or when you look towards something. They are always whispering in our ear, hoping we will hear them.

Ways the angels communicate.

1. Intuition, inspiration, epiphany.

The most common way they communicate is intuition, which includes thoughts, ideas, inspiration, and dreams.

Listening to our gut feeling or that little voice in our mind we usually argue with daily!

2. Feeling.

The angels are energy-light. They will reach out and touch our shoulders, put their hand on our back or softly touch our head. If you have ever felt a tingling sensation on your head – it is an angel caressing your hair. When you are struggling with overwhelming emotion, and you feel as if you are being hugged – smile, it is your angel!

3. Dreams.

The best time angels communicate with us is in our dreams; during that time, our conscious mind is not getting in the way – not second-guessing. Angels provide us with a wealth of information and guidance in our dreams. At night our inner self, our spirit knows no boundaries.

4. Feathers.

They leave feathers on our path. Angels know we are experiencing challenges, but they are always near supporting, loving, and guiding us, so they will put feathers down to remind us we are not alone on our journey.

5. Coins.

Angels will leave coins on our path to remind us we are precious and valuable. Every time I find money on the ground, I immediately say "Thank you!"

6. Sparkles or Orbs of Light.

They are sparkles, flashes, or orbs of light, a light in the corner of your eye. You may even see a figure in your peripheral vision. You are not hallucinating – it is an angel!

7. Smells or scents.

A smell or scent that reminds you of a loved one or that comforts you, yet there is no obvious source of the aroma. This is especially true when a loved one has passed away. Occasionally I will smell my daughters' perfume or favorite lotions which takes me to a special memory of her.

8. Rainbows and clouds.

Seeing a rainbow even if there was no rain. A double rainbow or a brightly colored rainbow is a sign of hope from the angels that all is well and going to turn out even better than you imagined. Unusual, shaped clouds are signs that we are loved, watched over and protected.

9. Butterflies, Dragonflies, or other creatures.

Seeing a creature, whether insect or animal, symbolizes something the angels are trying to tell you. For example, seeing a bluebird is a symbol of joy and happiness in the future; the bluebird is a symbol of the angelic realm. People around the world view the butterfly as a representation of endurance, change, hope, and life. The butterfly symbolizes great transformation and personal growth. The dragonfly symbolizes change, transformation, adaptability, and self-realization. The internet is a wonderful tool when you are searching for the meaning of seeing a creature often.

10. Communicate through other people.

Angels will send other people to help you with a situation or share experiences with you. Think about a time when you thought "if I only knew how to do this or knew someone who has done this and can help," and shortly after thinking that someone shows up and starts chatting with you: and amazingly they can help you.

11. Social Media.

Again, angels are energy, and because of this can send messages through our electronic devices. For example, hearing a song that reminds you of something specific, a billboard that gives an answer you have been seeking, a commercial, advertisements. This is especially true when we are grieving. I would get into my car, and the song that would be playing would remind me of my daughter – and it was the same song every time, "One Call Away" by Charlie Puth.

12. Buzzing noise in one or both ears.

If you have already had your ears examined by a doctor and there is nothing wrong medically, then it is your angel. Angels are downloading information and knowledge into your mind that you will be able to draw from in your future.

13. Voice.

If your Clairaudience (clear hearing) abilities are not developed, you will only hear the angels' voice in critical situations; for example, an angel rushes to rescue or warn you of impending danger. Angels communicate telepathically and will use a combination of psychic senses to reach us. They never give up and continually try different methods, hoping we will hear them.

14. Repeating Numbers (known as Angel Numbers).

When you see the same numbers repeated, this is Divine guidance. The angels are trying to get your attention. Numbers are the language of the universe, and each number has a meaning. Each number has a unique vibrational frequency, carrying messages that we can interpret.

Below are some of the Angel Number meanings. The repeating of numbers indicates more strength in the message.

111

A new spiritual journey awaits you. The energy around you right now is good for taking healthy risks, shifting patterns, or moving projects or relationships forward. Keep your eyes peeled for opportunities and take action steps that focus on your goals. Pay close attention to your ideas, beliefs, and feelings. Release what is worrying you and surround yourself with positive energy. This is your opportunity to create the future you desire. Your thoughts manifest your reality.

222

Work on establishing balance and harmony in your life. You must stay truthful and faithful to your personal beliefs. Seek what is missing from your life.

333

You need to learn to express yourself. Do not hold back. This is a sign of encouragement and strength and will give you the determination and persistence you need to move forward. This is several prayers answered, a reminder that the universe knows what you want and what you are working toward, and that you are being brought those opportunities and resources. You are being called to recognize your life purpose. Do not let doubt stop you from moving forward – you have got the universe on your side. You can overcome any obstacle in your path.

444

Your angels are encouraging you to reach for the stars. You are at a crossroads in your life and are starting to realize the importance of spirituality. You are on the right path. Do not give up and keep your eye on the prize. You are creating the groundwork for your dreams.

555

Major changes await you; embrace them. Personal growth or even physical change such as moving or finding a new job is in store. The universe is helping to pave the way for a new beginning; to move forward you must let go of something that is no longer serving you. You are attracting prosperity and wealth; keep your arms outstretched to continue receiving and integrating. Remember to trust that your angels are always giving you extra support.

66

You are stuck in the past; you must let go. This is the sign of encouragement that appears when you begin to lose faith in yourself. This number shows up when you are giving too much of yourself in a particular aspect of your life. You are a peace-bearer on a quest for truth and deep connection. Your empathic ability to heal others also helps you understand your own trauma and grief. Choose to provide care and kindness over service and sacrifice.

777

Your angels want to congratulate and encourage you. Embrace who you are and explore your hidden talents. It is a sign that spiritual evolution is upon you. Tap into your highest potential and embrace your individual gifts, using them to help the people around you. Keep going. Your relationship with Source is stronger and more meaningful now.

808

Trust in your abilities. Your angels are urging you to learn new things in order to progress.

818

Take control and pursue your dreams. Push the boundaries and realize your strength.

888

Something positive is on the way. You have the right mentality, and as a result, a world of possibilities will open up in whatever you choose to pursue. Abundance is your birthright. You naturally attract prosperity and find it easy to magnetize money and the opportunity to increase your wealth.

999

A chapter in your life is coming to an end. You need to focus on the bigger picture.

This phase in your life is coming to its natural conclusion, allowing you to make a fresh start. You will see that everything you have experienced and the lessons you have learned are helping you transform into who you are truly meant to be. You are here to help others ascend to higher levels of spiritual awareness.

0000

Your life is about to take a positive turn. Financial security is on the horizon, and your luck will change. It signifies a new beginning based on trust and belief outside rational thinking.

1010

Stop being complacent. A spiritual awakening is awaiting you. You have accomplished a full cycle and about to start a new one.

1111

Stop worrying about other people's opinions of you. A new and exciting beginning awaits you. A powerful new beginning, but this time you start your new project believing in yourself, feeling that you have got strength, knowledge, and confidence to make it a reality.

1212

Dream big and have faith in yourself. Stay positive and focus on the greater good. Time to view things from a different perspective and for fresh, bold, and revolutionary ideas.

1221

Use your positive attitude to go further. You are capable of great things, be optimistic and move forward.

1313

Ride the positive waves. Success is just around the corner; keep up the good work. The end of a painful situation. You start a new life from now on, or going through a transformation, the new you is about to be born.

1414

Concentrate on the positive aspects of life. Set your goals and focus on achieving them. Patience. Relax. Everything is going to happen in its own time.

2020

Things are changing for the better. Spiritually you are stepping on the path of Spiritual Awakening.

2121

Accept yourself for who you are. Evaluate your path and listen to your heart.

You are wise and experienced; you are finishing a journey and about to embark on another amazing one. A significant and exciting change in your life is coming.

2222

You must pause, get more information, consult someone – including angels and guides. Weigh the pros and cons of a situation. Ask angels for help – they really want to get in touch with you.

God surrounds us with a host of angels. Psalm 91:11-12, "For he will command his angels concerning you to guard you in all your ways; they will lift you up in their hands, so that you will not strike your foot against a stone." Exodus 23:20, "See, I am sending an angel ahead of you to guard you along the way and to bring you to the place I have prepared."

There are nine types of Angels.

1. Seraphim

They encircle God's throne and emit fiery light representing His love. They celebrate the praises of God's holiness and power. They act as the medium of communication between heaven and earth.

2. Cherub or Cherubim

These angels are the keepers of the celestial records and hold the knowledge of God.

3. Thrones

Their appearance is most bizarre. They are said to look like great glowing wheels covered with many eyes. They serve as God's chariot and dispense his judgment in order to carry out his desires for us.

4. Dominions or Dominations

Their primary purpose is to make sure that the cosmos remains in order by sending down power to heads of government and other authority figures.

5. Virtues

Shaped like sparks of light, Virtues are in charge of maintaining the natural world, and they inspire living things in areas such as science.

6. Powers

In celestial form, Powers appear like bright-colored, hazy fumes. Powers are border patrol agents between Heaven and Earth.

7. Principalities

These angelic beings are shaped like rays of light. They guide our entire world – nations, cities, and towns. They are also in charge of religion and politics.

8. Archangels

They are guardians of people and all things physical. Archangels respond best when dealing with matters involving all humankind.

9. Angels

They are true intermediaries between God and individual people. Angels do not watch over nations; they safeguard households and individuals who believe in God and keep them safe from demons. They nurture, counsel, and heal. We all have a "personal angel" or Guardian Angel with us daily.

Chapter 8 Reflection:

1. What is the purpose (intention) of the angels?

   _____

   _____

   _____

   _____

2. How do the angels communicate?

   _____

   _____

   _____

   _____

3. What are some ways the angels have communicated
   with
   you?_____

   _____

   _____

   _____

4. What are the nine types of angels?

   _____

   _____

   _____

   _____

   _____

Part 3

Personal Growth

Chapter 9

Faith

God does not forsake you, nor does He ever leave you. Deuteronomy 31:8 "The Lord himself goes before you and will be with you; he will never leave you nor forsake you." It is us who turn our backs or no longer listen; we start to question our intuition, our gut feelings. There are many reasons we may close our minds: suffering a tragedy or circumstances that make you doubt a higher being who 'watches' over you.

Let me take you back to the loss of my daughter as an excellent example of questioning or doubting.

The moment I got the news, I challenged God, asking how He could have allowed this beautiful girl, just beginning her life, to die. I wondered; what kind of God would do that? What reason would be significant enough to take her away? Then the questions turned to doubt: Does God even exist? A loving God would not do this, I thought.

The questions and doubts kept coming until I had enough. Standing in my kitchen, leaning against the counter, trying not to collapse to the floor from anguish. I yelled, "Enough!" through my tears. I then began with, "God, I don't know the reason for this tragedy, but I am thankful that I had 24 beautiful years with this incredible soul. I am mad at you, though, and for a while, I will not be talking with you. Just know I love you, and please keep my family and me safe as we go through this horror." Even though I began to question and doubt, I knew God was with me.

In questioning His existence, my inner being still brought me back to what Sunday School had taught me; I am loved. I did not know where to turn, but I knew I needed to hold on to the feeling that I was not alone through this pain. I was in anguish. We are His children and just as we get angry or filled with pain toward our parents – they are still there for us. They will patiently wait for us to talk with them. I knew that He would help me and not leave me just because I was sad and angry. He was there to comfort me and help me keep moving forward, one step at a time.

During that time, I did a lot of contemplation and research on the existence of God. I have always felt a higher or Divine presence – so that was not in question. I concluded that this Divine presence is called by many names throughout history and religious organizations. This presence acts on our behalf for the greatest good.

We may not understand or know this greater good but by aligning ourselves with this presence we are able to accomplish great things and overcome tragedies and obstacles in our life. But we will forever be changed. Overcoming a tragedy does not mean we no longer have lingering effects – how can someone truly overcome the loss of a loved one for example? We learn to deal with the pain and emptiness that loss brings. Hopefully, we say "I love you" more to those still here and show more love and compassion to those around us. Overcoming something simply means to succeed in dealing with the tragedy or obstacle.

What is faith?

Faith is full trust or belief in someone or something, a genuine belief in God, based on spiritual apprehension rather than proof.

I believe we all have faith. For example, we have confidence that our employer will give us a paycheck. We have faith that the company which installed the elevator in the building did it correctly, and that the mechanic who worked on our vehicle did an excellent job. Unfortunately, our faith usually does not flow outward.

All historical events are based on faith unless you were there and witnessed the event you are trusting the information you received is accurate.

When we choose not to listen to our intuition, decide not to walk with our Divine Spirit, we miss out on beautiful ideas. We miss out on opportunities that could propel our lives into abundance. Instead, we choose the roughest paths alone, even though God or Divine Spirits are trying to guide us down a safer, more prosperous road.

The universe is full of possibilities and tapping into the universal consciousness that exists through a spiritual connection with nature, people and the earth helps bring out our full potential. We are not alone, and we can overcome any obstacle placed in our path by seeking the knowledge in our subconscious mind and the universe.

Faith is trusting what you cannot see will come to pass. Faith attracts the positive, while fear attracts the negative. People with faith work with the little they have rather than waiting for the abundance they are receiving.

The evidence that we are using faith is in our works. Faith is a belief in action.

What is Belief?

The decisions we make are different when we know what is important to us; we manage each day to be and do what matters most. You are already doing what you are uncomfortable doing, by changing your focus to what is important, you become excited changing your perception into believing you can realize your dream and you can move mountains. The people you deal with now will still be the same people you always deal with later; the faces may change, but the personalities will not.

Picture a rock tumbler for a moment. You put the rough stones in, and by the time it is complete, you have polished shiny rocks. It takes time, but the hard edges get smoothed away. Now, picture yourself as unpolished stones. You will become polished as you traverse through your life's journey.

Our God, Divine Spirit, is smoothing away all the rough edges. Learning to listen to our intuition is the best way the universe, God, or Divine Spirits speak with us. We will learn either way – it just may take more time. We learn through relationships with others, through turmoil and tragedy, and from subconscious realization. Whatever way we are most receptive is the way we will get the information or lessons. We become humble and then shaped into the person we are meant to be. Not the person we have settled for being.

I find this interesting: when we are thirsty – on the edge of dehydration – we do not believe we are parched. It is the same way with everything in our lives. If we are on the verge of poverty, we do not realize we are in trouble. We think 'if I just stay at my job for a few more years, things will get better.' We reassure ourselves.

While living in Alaska, I visited the zoo and noticed the bears pacing back and forth. I asked one of the rangers why they walk back and forth.

He said, when the bear is in captivity, they go insane and therefore begin to move back and forth. I find that interesting, and believe it correlates with our thought patterns of not realizing we are in trouble. We get up, go to work, go home; the next day, we get up, go to work, go back home. Thinking something will miraculously change.

What on earth makes a person think that way? Simple, society teaches us that it is normal. It does not get better; you give up on your life, your dreams, and your happiness. How exactly is that good?! We can do, have, and aspire for anything we dream. It has always been in our reach; being taught that is not reality. Reality is a concept that can box us into a specific mindset or allow us to spread our wings – it is our choice. I recently read, "You came here to create reality-not to accept it."

We rush through life only to realize in the end that we did not have a chance to live. Where are you right now? Are you just starting a family? Are your children just starting school or graduating? Are your kids starting their own families? How much time have they had with you? Or have you been so busy, one day you woke up to realize they were not around as often or at all? For things to change, to become better, you need to know where you are right now.

As we grow older, we become harder; we do this to protect ourselves. We shelter our family and ourselves. The intention is to protect them when, in reality, we are stealing any dreams and desires they may have. We put blinders on and all the opportunities that we had, or have, we no longer recognize. The things we see, we analyze until we are positive, we could get hurt, or disaster is just around the corner. At that moment, we decide not to try.

We are not here to be cowards going through life. We are here to explore, to grow with the enthusiasm we once had. Yes, there could be a danger, most likely there is, and yes, we may get hurt, but that is what makes us know we are alive – feelings, sensations. We are not to stuff our emotions away because it is not convenient. We are to live, to feel, to grow. Otherwise, we should just as well lock ourselves in a cage and throw away the key. We lock ourselves in our house and do not come out until we must go back to work, hurry to our job, and then home, to do it all over again the next day.

Let us look, for a moment, at the birds. They get pushed out of their nest while learning to fly. Is that dangerous? I think so. Do some get hurt? Absolutely, but they learn to fly. Most people have never left their nest, spread their wings, and soared. They have just hopped to another nest. The universe allows you to fly! FLY!

We have been trained, taught, to find a good job and stay there until we retire so we can collect retirement for security. Why is that what we are instructed to do? That is the wrong perspective. We are to spread our wings, to feel the wind rushing over our face, to soar. We can touch lives, give hope, and show love and kindness. What makes you think you are to do anything less? Can you touch lives, give hope, and show compassion with the job you are currently employed? Yes. Not as dynamically as God or the universe wants; otherwise, He would have said get a job and stay put – do not expand or grow. Quite the contrary, we are always being stretched. I laugh at the saying "God only gives you what you can handle," apparently, He has a tremendous amount of faith in my capabilities! So much more than I do.

Inside every person is a mighty and powerful spirit. The difference is how we unleash it. As a child, it would shine through glorious little eyes; now, we must look deep into those same eyes and pray, we can still see it. Years of negative influences (Do not! Cannot! No!) cover the glimmer of hope, the excitement, and the child's strong determination. How will you unleash that child and begin to have the things you always knew, in your heart, you should have?

The number of people who eagerly wait to say you cannot do something is astonishing. I genuinely believe the moment you think of something that few have thought these people come out of the woodwork. Negative people are everywhere. They lurk in hallways; they are always around the corner. I do not believe they are decisively trying to discourage you. Most of them are saying this because they do not want to see you get hurt, or they are looking out for you – they have your best interest at heart.

I once told a close friend about one of my dreams and stated at my current rate; I would not reach it in a reasonable amount of time. She told me I should change my goal, be more realistic. That statement broke my heart, not because I believed she was right, but because that is what she started doing.

Do not change your goals and dreams because you do not have the money or time. You must find the right vehicle to get you to your dreams and goals. Settling for something you did not want will never make you happy. Something inside begins to die; perhaps it is your ambition, maybe even your will. Once you have made a conscious decision to go for your dream you will begin to create inertia. The more you think about your dreams will thrust you into achieving your desires.

Remember, listening to foolish people shows disrespect for yourself.

Next time you hear that comment, ask them what they think your best interests are. What they are saying is simple: You cannot possibly know what is best for you or your family, so we are here to help you. Please do not misunderstand; there are certain circumstances where a friend may have a better view, but it all comes down to perception. How you perceive a situation is VASTLY different than a friend, even though you both are close.

For example, in high school, my best friend and I went to the mall. We were meeting her family at McDonald's for lunch. Her mother asked us if we wanted to sit with them or at a table by ourselves. Of course, we chose a table by ourselves (we were teenagers!). Her mother was distraught with us, as she thought we all wanted to sit together.

How we perceive something undoubtedly impacts our reaction. Remember: You can do everything you set your mind to do. Our thoughts are powerful if we only use them positively. Thinking positively takes less energy. Remember: for every negative thought or comment it takes ten positive statements to wipe away that single thought. Negativity drains the positive and creates division.

Look deep within yourself. Glory is only a decision away. First, decide to find that child's spirit and your dreams. Second, ask yourself: Am I willing to work for my goals with the raw determination of the child I once was? After doing that, the rest is easy. You may have obstacles to overcome, but if you stay the course, your reward will be great.

What do you need to do to find it? When did it start disappearing? Perhaps the first time someone you idolized said you could not do that or get your head out of the clouds — dream stealers. You must decide no one can touch your dreams; they have no say in your abilities.

GO FOR IT! You CAN do it!

Let's go back to your yesteryears. Do you remember your first love? How hard did you work in reaching the ultimate goal: a relationship, closeness? You can use that same determination for yourself and your family today. You are the only one that can move beyond the temptation to hold yourself back.

The journey will have obstacles to help you grow, to help you reach your potential. We all go over them, around them, through them. Just do it! You deserve all that you work towards and all that you desire, do not settle for anything less.

We all have gifts and abilities or talents – something we excel and enjoy doing. Does your job enhance or hinder your gifts? If it blocks them, get a new job. These gifts and talents are from God, your Divine Spirit, the universe; when we use them, we feel the energy, excitement, and joy.

I have heard we are lowly, not worthy of Divine blessings. Shame on all those who say that! Make no mistake; we are worthy of all the miracles the universe has to offer. Eternal life is a quality of life. We have it now – we should be living that way.

It is easier to believe someone else than to seek the information yourself. Most of the time, when you are looking something up, it means a great deal to you and is directly affecting you. Thus, having someone else look, you remove yourself from the pain, as a buffer.

As you tap into your subconscious mind and the universal consciousness, you become more aware of your true-life purpose, your blessings, and your abilities. A new world will open to you.

A dream does not become a goal until it is written down. Dreams are wonderful, we all have them, but the significance of putting them on paper and setting a goal to accomplish them – you begin to get recharged, energetic. Your excitement and zest for life will increase. There is power in turning a dream into a goal and working towards it. You are only committed to what you acknowledge, believe what you have written down. Dreaming without doing is folly. To change your conduct, you must first change your beliefs.

The more your perceptions align with truth, the more prosperous you become as the truthfulness sets you free. Remember, what you think in your heart determines what you become. What you believe will either attract or repel what you desire, dream. Your beliefs bind you, and the yoke you wear defines the burden you bear.

Principals are essential truths, fundamental laws of the universe, facts of nature, and primary units of life. Discerning principles is a lifelong passion for people who succeed. The more you build your life on faith, the higher your highs, the straighter your path, and the greater your life will become. You become successful and prosper when you base your life on principles and find the patterns that work for you.

Chapter 9 Reflection:

1. What is faith?_____
   _____
   _____

2. What brings out a person's full potential?
   _____
   _____

3. Have you ever questioned or doubted God?
   _____
   _____
   _____

4. Have you been able to move past the doubt?
   _____ If so, How?_____
   _____

5. What is belief?_____
   _____
   _____

6. We learn through:

   a. _____
   b. _____
   c. _____

7. What is your reality?_____
   _____
   _____
   _____

8. Do you feel boxed in or able to spread your wings?
   _____

9. Listening to foolish people shows
   _____

10. You can do:_____

_____

11. Negativity drains

_____ & creates

_____.

Chapter 10

True Self

Understanding yourself (the part of you that very few people see) will help you open to the knowledge and wisdom of the universal consciousness and God. Allowing you to find the method that works best for you.

There are two core beliefs regarding a person's true self: morality and goodness. An individual's true self influences their judgments and actions that give their life meaning.

Truth is the one moral, ethical, and correct foundation that exists for a strong character. Opinions will not hold up to the truth. Truth must be sought, studied, and learned to develop good character; without this quality, all accomplishments are short-lived.

We must learn about our true selves, meditate on it, hold it as a valued and cherished treasure, to develop and maintain a strong character, which translates into societal order and peaceful living.

Here are four ways to recognize your true self.

1. Listen to your inner voice.

Listening will help you become conscious of and recognize your true self with honesty. It enables you to realize your wants, desires, likes, and dislikes without limitations or judgment.

2. Give yourself the freedom to be you.

Let go of comparisons, labels, status, and criticisms. Giving yourself this freedom allows you to empower who you truly are within and provide you with strength and courage.

3. Allow changes to be made.

Changing the items around you to be more in tune with your likes will reflect what you are feeling within, it reinforces the freedom to express your true self.

4. Learn to trust yourself.

Trust your initial choices and decisions. Trusting yourself will give you the will power and courage to continue pursuing what is in your heart.

Lies and all that is morally wrong, inconsistent with good character and destructive to morals and society, are never right. They only lead to pain and torment.

Honesty is the key because when truth collapses, morality has nothing on which to stand. Truth stands the test of time. Truth is a person's unassailable and unyielding basis for good character. Telling the truth might be one of the hardest things you will ever do, but once you do it, it is the most exhilarating. The enlargement of the heart, freedom from guilt, and absence of anxiety is well worth the price of a moment of discomfort.

Deepak Chopra, MD, in his book "How to Tell the Difference Between Your True Self and Your Everyday Self" states:

Your true self is certain and clear.

Your true self is stable.

Your true self is driven by a deep sense of truth.

Your true self is at peace.

Your true self is love.

Qualities of your true self are self-reliant, evolutionary, loving, creative, knowing, accepting, and peaceful.

Acknowledging your true self will enable you to achieve an amazing life. We have all heard the saying, "if your mind can conceive it, and your heart believes it, you can achieve it." When you dream, write your vision, or dream down. Focus on your strengths, believe you are going to prosper, it is your heart that will carry you or condemn you.

What you believe in your heart affects what you will become. Whatever you meditate on, focus on, and concentrate on will eventually drop from your head to your heart. Align your focus on your true self, and that which ignites excitement throughout your whole body. Feeding your mind and soul with truth and encouraging words, your heart and mind will start to prosper, and external financial prosperity and abundance in all aspects of your life will come.

The person you genuinely are will come out when you are face to face with tragedy. I pondered on that for a while. Think about that statement! If you are generous in the good times, you will be more generous in the bad times. If you love in the good times, you will be more loving in the bad times. If you are angry in the good times, you will be more upset in the bad times. Your character, your true self, will come out exponentially in the bad times.

I found that statement to be accurate when I lost my daughter. I poured love onto others. I wanted to help whoever needed help. In my pain, I chose to reach out because it made me feel better – I looked beyond my pain and perhaps eased someone else's a little. Focusing on helping others, I was able to move beyond my sadness for a little while and give encouragement and love to another. We all need that at some point in our lives.

Chapter 10 Reflection:

1. Understanding yourself will help you:
   _____ & _____.

2. What are your attributes (Your unchanging qualities)?

   _____

   _____

   _____

3. What is your character?_____

   _____

   _____

4. How would you describe who you are?

   _____

   _____

5. Ask a friend to describe who you are to them.
6. What are the two core beliefs of true self?

   _____

   _____

7. How can you recognize your true self?

   _____

   _____

8. List the qualities of your true self.

   _____

   _____

9. Finish this sentence, your true self is...

   a. _____
   b. _____
   c. _____
   d. _____
   e. _____

Chapter 11

Vibrational Energy

Vibrational Energy is in everything. This energy is essential, and it can either be positive energy or negative energy around you. Raising your vibration will bring you into a more positive state of being.

There are several ways you can increase your vibrational energy. Here are a few examples:

- Gemstones –

  The very nature and energy of gems is a universal energy. Each one has a unique vibration that can help in the healing process and well-being of the user. The basic vibrational pattern is in all physical phenomena, from electromagnetic waves to ripples in the water, or the finite movement of electrons. Each stone is both a transmitter and a receiver of various vibrations, which vibrates and emits its unique radiance. This radiance interacts with the electromagnetic field of our bodies. For example, Amethyst encourages cleansing processes during sleep and intensifies dreams, it also helps ease pain and assists an individual's inner self in strengthening; Rose Quartz is known as the love stone, helps with love, brings compassion and self-esteem – it calms and soothes.

- Essential Oils or Aromas –

    Highly concentrated plant extracts. They have been used in Ancient Greece, Ancient Egypt, India, and China. Fragrances help to balance the body's systems, strengthen, and support the immune system, provide relief from pain, calm the nervous system, and so much more. I use a blend of essential oils daily for anxiety and grief. For example, eucalyptus is great as a decongestant; lavender has a positive effect on both body and mind – it has anti-inflammatory and antiseptic properties and has a calming, balancing systems, and relaxing qualities.

    Have you ever been walking, and you smell a sweet fragrance that immediately brings a smile to your face or you remember something from your past? Aromas can help calm your mind and open up your senses, which helps to raise your vibrational energies.

- Vibrational frequencies.

    The vibrational frequencies come from an ancient six tone scale (these are the primary frequencies). Each one has a unique tone required to balance your energy, keep your body, mind, and spirit in perfect harmony. They are called the Solfeggio frequencies.

Nikola Tesla stated, "If you want to find the secrets of the Universe, think in terms of energy, frequency, and vibration."

"Emotions are what make us human. Make us real. The word emotion stands for energy in motion. Be truthful about your emotions and use your mind and emotions in your favor, not against yourself." - Robert Kyosaki

"Energy doesn't come to us so much from the things around us-although we can absorb energy directly from some plants and sacred sites. Sacred energy comes from our connection to the divine inside us." – James Redfield

Raising your vibration, at first, can feel like you are on a roller coaster. Learning to live on a higher vibrational frequency takes time to create your new normal vibration. For example, you have just begun raising your vibration, and a close friend comes up to you terribly upset. Your vibration may lower because their vibration is low; this will frequently happen for a while until you have been on a higher frequency for a couple of weeks. As you consciously begin to raise your vibrational energies the negativities of the world will not affect you as much, or even at all.

The six main Solfeggio frequencies are 396 Hz, 417 Hz, 528 Hz, 639 Hz, 741 Hz, 852 Hz.

Today we know them as Do-Re-Mi-Fa-So-La-Ti. Sound familiar? Every time I think of these notes, it reminds me of the movie Sound of Music with Julie Andrews! Do is also referred to as UT.

(DO) UT – 396 Hz

This is associated with the Root Chakra. It is the tone of the Earth's Day; dynamic, energizing and vitalizing. This frequency helps turn grief into joy and liberates guilt and fear. It cleanses the feeling of guilt. Seeks out hidden blockages, subconscious negative beliefs, and ideas that have led to your present situations. This vibrational tone liberates energy and enables you to achieve your goals in the most direct way.

RE – 417 Hz

This is associated with the Sacral Chakra; the tone of the synodic moon (Lunar month). This frequency helps cleanse traumatic experiences and clears the harmful influences of past events. On the cellular level, this tone encourages the cell and its functions optimally. You are in touch with an inexhaustible source of energy that allows you to change your life. It produces power to bring about change.

MI – 528 Hz

This tone is associated with the Solar Plexus Chakra. MI is the frequency of the sun. This tone is utilized to return human DNA to its original, perfect state. Beneficial effects follow the process of DNA reparation – an enhanced amount of life energy, clarity of mind, consciousness, awakened or activated creativity, ecstatic states like deep inner peace, dance, and celebration. MI activates your imagination, intention, and intuition to operate for your highest and best purpose.

FA – 639 Hz

This is associated with the Heart Chakra, the tone of the Earth's year. FA 639 Hz enables the creation of a harmonious community and harmonious interpersonal relationships. Listen to FA when dealing with relationship problems. On a cellular level, 639 Hz can be used to encourage the cell to communicate with its environment. This frequency enhances communication, understanding, tolerance, and love.

SO – 741 Hz

This is associated with the Throat Chakra, the tone of the planet Mercury. Cleans the cell (Solve Polluti) from toxins. SOL cleans the cell from different kinds of electromagnetic radiations. Also, this frequency is solving problems of any nature. It will also lead you into the power of self-expression, which results in a pure and stable life. This tone intends to solve and cleanse.

LA – 852 Hz

This is associated with the Third Eye Chakra; the tone of the planet Venus. This frequency improves your ability to see through the hidden agendas of people, places, and things (illusions) of your life. It is a means for opening a person up for communication with the all-embracing Spirit. On a cellular level, it enables the cell to transform itself into a system of higher level. Raising awareness and allows you to return to spiritual order.

TI – 963 Hz

This is associated with the Crown Chakra, the tone of the Platonic Year or Great Year. This frequency stimulates any system to its original perfect state. It is related to the Light and all-embracing Spirit and enables direct experience, the return of Oneness. It re-connects you with the Spirit or the non-vibrational energies of the spiritual world. It will empower you to experience Oneness-our true nature.

174 – Hz

This frequency appears to be a natural anesthetic. It helps to lessen pain physically and energetically. This frequency gives your organs a sense of security, safety, and love, encouraging them to do their best.

285 – Hz

This frequency helps return the tissue to its original form. It impacts energy fields, delivering a message for restructuring injured organs. Your body is rejuvenated and energized.

7.83– Hz

This is known as the Schumann Resonance and is the frequency of Earth. It was discovered in 1952 by physicist

Dr. Winfried Otto Schumann. This frequency helps us sync with the Earth's frequency. If we are not in sync with Earths frequency, we begin to show signs of discomfort: anxiety, insomnia, illness, suppressed immune system, etc. Tuning into this frequency allows the body to heal and increases vitality.

Chapter 11 Reflection:

1. What are some ways you can raise your vibration?

   _____

   _____

   _____

2. Have you ever been drawn to a certain gemstone?

   _____

   _____

3. What are essential oils?_____

   _____

   _____

4. Fragrances help:

   a. _____

   b. _____

   c. _____

   d. _____

5. What are the six Solfeggio frequencies?

   _____

   _____

   _____

6. What is the Schumann Resonance?

   _____

   _____

   _____

Chapter 12

Chakras

Chakras are energy centers in the body. There are seven significant centers through the middle of the body that focuses on specific frequencies. The Chakras maintain a healthy balance throughout your body. If one of the energy centers is disrupted or blocked, your body will not be as healthy as it should and usually shows as physical, emotional, or spiritual problems.

The word Chakra originated from the Sanskrit texts and means the wheel. They are responsible for the smooth flow of energy from one part of the body to another.

The Chakras help you connect emotionally, physically, and spiritually.

The seven universal Chakras are:

1. Root Chakra (in Sanskrit: Muladhara)

Location: the base of the spine.

Associated color: Red. This color is associated with healing bones and bone marrow.

It governs the adrenal glands.

It symbolizes safety, survival, grounding, and nourishment from the Earth's energy. The origin of sexual energy and vitality. This chakra governs kidneys, bladder, hips. The Root Chakra tends to mankind's basic needs, such as safety, survival, security, and energy distribution.

If this Chakra is out of balance, you may experience fear, insecurity, and anxiety.

2. Sacral Chakra (Swadhisthana)

Location: the lower abdomen, below the navel.

Associated color: Orange. The color orange is related to glands and adrenals.

It governs the stomach and related organs such as the male and female primary sexual organs.

It symbolizes creativity, feelings, sexual drive, pleasure, and exploration. It is responsible for a person's will and desire to succeed.

If this Chakra is blocked, you may become emotionally manipulative.

3. Solar Plexus Chakra (Manipura)

Location: Just below the ribcage.

Associated color: Yellow. This color is related to the nervous system.

It governs liver, spleen, small intestines, and pancreas.

It symbolizes mental activities, intellect, personal power, and will.

This Chakra is associated with confidence, sound temperament and the ability to use one's intelligence in an effective manner, sense of identity, and personal power.

If this Chakra is blocked, you may experience ulcers, pancreatitis, depression, and excessive worry.

4. Heart Chakra (Anahata)

Location: center of the chest.

Associated color: Green. This color is related to the lungs and lung tissue.

It is connected to the thymus gland and governs your immunity, ability to feel love and compassion, as well as the ability to forgive, relationships, personal development, direction, and sharing. You may be sympathetic, generous, humble, and romantic.

5. Throat Chakra (Vishuddha)

Location: Throat.

Associated color: Blue. This color is for optimal bodily functions.

It controls the thyroid gland.

This Chakra helps you become more tactful, inspiring, and loyal. It also helps with communication, personal expression, and the flow of information.

It symbolizes self-expression, expression of truth, creative expression, and communication.

If this Chakra is out of balance, you may experience bronchitis, asthma, or tonsillitis.

6. Brow or Third Eye Chakra (Ajna)

Location: center of the forehead.

Associated color: Purple or Deep Indigo Blue. This color is for fascia and skin.

It is associated with the pituitary gland, eyes, and sinuses.

It helps you become fearless, wise, truth-seeking, intuitive, understanding, perceptive, knowledge, and mental organization. It evokes intuition, extrasensory perception, and inner wisdom.

7. Crown Chakra (Sahasrara)

Location: above the top of the head.

Associated color: White.

It is associated with the pineal gland.

It symbolizes the universal connection with spirituality and consciousness. It maintains the overall balance of the Chakra system and channels universal life energy into the system. It also supports a sense of wholeness and stimulates fine levels of perception, intuition, and inspiration.

If this Chakra is well balanced, you may be mentally strong and creative.

As a chakra accumulates stress, it becomes less able to absorb and direct the appropriate energy into the body, creating an imbalance in your body. At this point, you will need to cleanse your chakras. You can do that by using a clear crystal quartz gemstone pendulum at each chakra. Hold the pendulum at each location, letting it move freely for a couple of minutes before moving to the next area. This is a basic way to rebalance. There are more in-depth ways, but I have found this to be effective for a quick rebalance until I can spend more time on each chakra.

The Chakra colors reflect different frequencies of light and energy. The colors are based on modern healing methods.

Each Chakra also has gemstones associated with them, and pairing gems with the Chakras will increase unity and help with healing.

Healing Stones for the Chakras

Root – Red gemstones such as Agates (Fire Agate), Bloodstone, Hematite, Tigers Eye.

Sacral – Orange gems can be used, such as Carnelian, Citrine, and Coral.

Solar Plexus – Yellow gems such as Calcite, Citrine, Malachite, and Topaz.

Heart – Green gems such as Green Calcite, Green Tourmaline, Jade, and Rose Quartz.

Throat – Blue gems can be used such as Aquamarine, Lapis Lazuli and Turquoise.

Third Eye – Indigo or Purple gemstones can be used such as Amethyst, Black Obsidian and Purple Flourite.

Crown – Purple or White gemstones such as Amethyst, Diamond, Clear Quartz and Selenite.

Chapter 12 Reflection:

1. What are Chakras?_____
   _____
   _____

2. How do chakras help you?
   _____
   _____
   _____

3. What area of the body does each chakra govern?
   _____
   _____
   _____

4. What are the associated colors for each chakra?
   _____
   _____
   _____

5. What does accumulated stress do to chakras?
   _____
   _____
   _____

Chapter 13

Focus

I was sitting at my table, preparing my daily Bible study. My thoughts over the past few months had been racing, a blur on my subconscious. I started feeling overwhelmed, perhaps even defeated, out of control. A few moments more and a thought came to me – clear and concise. I tried to pass over it until it became louder.

The thought was simplistic – FOCUS. I needed to focus, but on what? There were so many thoughts going through my mind. Then it came swiftly, and my thoughts quieted. Focus on spirituality.

Focus always on spirituality. Release all your turmoil, your sadness – give all of it over to God, to the universe, asking that it be reconstructed in light and love.

"Brothers and sisters, I do not consider myself yet to have taken hold of it. But one thing I do: Forgetting what is behind and straining toward what is ahead, I press on toward the goal to win the prize for which God has called me heavenward in Christ Jesus." Philippians 3:13-14

How do you become focused on God?

1. Read daily.

Expand your understanding of the universe.

    a. If you are a Christian: Read your Bible daily. I have had numerous people come up to me and say, "No one has ever taught me how to read the Bible." So, they do not. They are trusting another to give them God's instruction for their lives. Open your heart and mind to the teachings in the Bible. You must first open it and begin reading. You do not have to start at Genesis; this is not an ordinary book you read cover to cover. The Bible is a collection of many books put together. So, pick one of these books and read them. Take one chapter at a time. As you hunger to learn how to do in-depth studies – someone will come into your life at that time to help you. God will provide you with mentors to help you on your journey. Proverbs 24:5-6 tells us, "A wise man is strong, yes, a man of knowledge increases strength; For by wise counsel, you will wage your own war, and in a multitude of counselors there is safety."

    b. Whatever your beliefs are, read the books, the histories that help expand your knowledge.

2. Prayer/Meditation

Take time in quiet reflection. Give yourself time to rejuvenate.

3. Thankfulness.

Acknowledge the little things; the bird that is singing outside your window. Appreciate the roof over your head, your family, and friends. I end each day saying, "Thank You!" seven times. (Sometimes more when my day has been exceedingly trying!) I have noticed that this also helps me to see more things to be thankful for daily.

4. Follow through.

Whatever information you get from the universe, follow through with it. Give it everything you have. Your rewards will be endless. We all love getting acknowledged for a job well done. The reward or blessing is a raise, perhaps a promotion. We also get rewards from the universe.

5. Praise

Thank the universe, God, Divine Spirits, Guides for what they are doing in your life. You are unique.

As you walk down your path of life, where is your focus? Are you focused on what you could stumble over, or are you looking forward to where you are heading? I have heard people say many times, 'I have stumbled again' or 'I just can't seem to get past this point in my life.' Why? Because they are not focusing on the end, with the end in mind your stumbling blocks, the obstacles you face, will not appear as ominous. You will not get the 'poor me' attitude.

How do you focus on the end first? Take a few steps back, sit down. Now ask yourself these simple questions and do not get up until you have answered them:

1. Where do I want to be?
2. How do I get there?
3. What do I need to accomplish this?
4. What must I do first?

Turn the stumbling blocks into steppingstones and move forward. You got this!

People become cynical because of the way others have treated them regarding their dreams and hopes. Let me give you an example: My grandmother was known to be one of the orneriest people in the family. (At a family reunion, I had someone come up to me and say, "Is this your Grandma?" After affirming that she was, they said "I am so sorry, she has always been cruel.") I wanted to understand what had happened in her life that would make her so bitter, so I began asking her and other family members questions. What I found was tragic! She was the oldest of ten children. Her mother died suddenly (when my Grandmother was a teenager), and she took the role of raising her younger siblings. Her father (in his grief) became an alcoholic, so she also had to take care of him as well. She married Grandpa at eighteen and moved her siblings in with them. Her first child, a beautiful baby girl who died three days after she was born.

Grandma ended up having two more children, and they moved to Montana after her youngest sibling graduated. I left out a lot of painful memories, but you get the idea. She learned early on it was not worth dreaming. She lost all hope and had become bitter. Once, she told my mother, "You shouldn't always be so positive because you will only get hurt." Terribly sad.

Chapter 13 Reflection:

1. What is your primary focus?_____

    _____

    _____

    _____

2. Is it in line with what you believe is your life
   purpose?

    _____

3. Where do you want you want to be?

    _____

    _____

    _____

4. How do you get there?

    _____

    _____

    _____

5. What do you need to accomplish this?

    _____

    _____

    _____

6. What must you do first?

    _____

    _____

    _____

Chapter 14

Humility

Humility is such a misunderstood word. People believe in having true humility; you will have nothing. Humility is how we perceive things and react. We do not have to lose everything before we can have humility. Unfortunately, for most, that is true. When they have lost everything, this is the only time they will open their hearts and begin looking at life from an unfamiliar perspective.

An excellent definition of humility is the quality of being humble. Dictionaries state humility is a low self-regard and a sense of worthiness. No wonder humility is such a misunderstood word! Humility is an outward expression of a genuine inner spirit or self-regard. People usually associate humility with humiliation, which is an imposition, often external, of shame upon a person.

Humility means submission. "Likewise, you younger people, submit yourselves to your elders. Yes, all of you be submissive to one another, and be clothed with humility, for 'God resists the proud, but give grace to the humble.'"

1 Peter 5:5-6. We are not to be proud and so high up that we are unable to accept correction or exhortation. We should not think that our opinions are always better than others.

Humility also does not mean we should be silent or be passive. We should possess a gentle and quiet spirit, as God desires. The importance of being humble and quiet our minds is so we may hear the Divine Spirit speaking to us throughout the day. Being humble does not mean we should hold our tongue when we see a situation where we should be bold and speak up.

Having a humble mindset is to think soberly about oneself. Meaning we do not boast of our accomplishments and abilities. "For by the grace given to me, I say to everyone among you not to think of himself more highly than he ought to think, but to think with sober judgment, each according to the measure of faith that God has assigned." Romans 12:3.

Jesus is the ultimate model of humility. He did not value His self-importance or honor.

Chapter 14 Reflection:

1. What is the importance of being humble?

   _____

   _____

   _____

2. Humility is an outward expression of

   _____

   _____

   _____

3. What is having a humble mindset?

   _____

   _____

   _____

Chapter 15

Prayer/Meditation

A correct basis for asking for something from our God or the Angels gives them a reason to answer your prayers, which means to pray with pure intentions, not to cause pain.

How can we say we spend enough time in prayer and meditation when we are always in a hurry? We have no study time, no solitude. We rush through prayer or meditation with a subconscious timer set as if it were a duty, a task to be crossed off when completed.

We stifle our inner being, our spiritual connection, and the wisdom the universe can give us. We do not allow ourselves time to release the negativity and stresses to the universe; instead, we have chosen to carry them with us wherever we travel. Calming our minds, listening to our inner self, and drawing from the wisdom of the universe will help each of us find peace, answers, and love.

There are several ways to pray and meditate, and there is no right or wrong way. People assume everyone knows how to – you start! Yes, you can start, but to say that to someone just beginning is like telling a baby to start talking.

When I first began attending church, I was timid and critical of myself – especially when it came to prayer. My thoughts were: what if I mess up the prayer, will God not listen to me or judge me based on my inability to talk to Him the right way? A thousand thoughts would run through my mind!

One day the pastor's wife heard I was going through a tough time and asked if she could pray with me. Of course, I thought, wonderful! She knows how to pray, and I can learn from her! I never prayed out loud; I was scared, thinking I would not pray correctly and be judged. At the end of her praying with me, she said, "Next time you should join me in the prayer." Again, my mind raced! I was right there with you! You asked to pray with me!" I was now timid, scared, and embarrassed! My point is, we do not know what is going on with someone – the inner turmoil they may be going through. Relax. The best way to pray is to simply begin talking to God as you would your best friend. He does not judge you on how eloquently you pray – He is elated that you are communicating with Him!

First, find a quiet place where you usually go for comfort. Then, relax; as a thought comes to mind, picture a basket beside you and place it in the basket. At first, your basket will appear to be the only thing that you are working on, but within a couple of weeks, your mind will begin to relax. You will start to have clarity and peace. You will start to think of people or circumstances that have been on your mind – pray for each one.

Prayer Time.

1. Location: a quiet place.
2. Keep a prayer journal and have a section for prayers and answered prayers.
3. Include praise and thanksgiving daily.
4. Daily – ask God to join you as you pray and to stay with you throughout your day. Pray for family, friends, your work, those that are traveling, etc. Think about those you would like to pray for daily.
5. Weekly – select items to prayer for each day of the week, for example, on Sunday pray for Churches and Church Leaders, Monday pray for Groups and Church unity, and so on. Some weekly prayer suggestions are My Home, Nations, Missions and Organizations, Ministries, Governments, Social Justice, Media, Extended Families, and Finances.
6. Ask for forgiveness. We are not perfect, and we make mistakes.

In meditation, do not try to stifle your thoughts. Observe them – both the positive and negative ones. Do not fight to wash the negative ones away; do not focus on them. It is ok to have those thoughts pass by as we learn. The problem that usually comes up is that we focus intently on the negative and forget the positive. As you observe your thoughts, you will begin to see things clearer. You are not in the fray of your reflections but sitting on a bench-watching. Allow your mind to wander as you observe; by doing this, your subconscious will begin to open to your true potential.

As you begin to quiet your mind and relax, you will soon start to get revelations concerning your life and the direction you should go. You will hear and acknowledge your inner voice, your intuition. A bond with something greater than yourself will start to form.

You will begin to see and appreciate things around you more. You will have an inner peace through any situation.

Chapter 15 Reflection:

1. What is the correct basis for asking God for something?

   _____

   _____

2. Do you have a special place to pray and meditate?

   _____

   _____

3. What is your prayer time or meditation like?

   _____

   _____

Chapter 16

Bible Study

The Bible is not like a regular book where you start on Chapter 1 and continue to the end. It is made up of several books. Seeking a personal relationship with God, it is best to understand who He is, His love and compassion first. Begin your studies with the Gospels. Then study the Books of History, the Books of Law, and the Books of Poetry. However, the way you choose to begin exploring the Bible is the right way.

I recommend getting a Bible that is easy to read and understand. One of my favorites is the NIV Bible or Young Explorer's Bible. I will have 2 Bibles (Scofield Bible and NIV Bible) with me while I study-one for reading and the other for research. The Scofield Bible has a section on each page, referencing other verses in the Bible.

First, I read the Scofield Bible verse, then read the NIV Bible verse, from the Scofield I will then look up the verse references using the NIV. I take notes on the Bible verse, then move on to the next verse.

Here is an example:

1. I gather my study journal, my Bibles, and my pen. I will write the verse in my journal.

John 14:27 (Scofield) Peace* I leave with you, my* peace I give unto you; not as the world* giveth, give I unto you. Let not your heart be troubled*, neither let it be afraid.

John 14:27 (NIV-Young Explorer's) Peace I leave with you; my peach I give you. I do not give to you as the world gives. Do not let your hearts be troubled and do not be afraid.

2. Research the asterisks or references from the Scofield. I will write each reference verse under the verse I am studying.

Peace* - (Matthew 10:34 note – because this is in the notes, it is in the Scofield Bible) Peace is spoken of in Scripture in three ways: (1) "Peace with God" (Romans 5:1); (2) "The peace of God" (Phil 4:7); inward peace, the state of the soul of that believer who, having entered into peace with God through faith in Christ, has also committed to God through prayer and supplication with thanksgiving all his anxieties (Lk 7:50; Phil 4.6). (3) Peace "on earth" (Lk 2:14; Psa 72:7; Psa 85:10; Isa 9:6, 7; Isa 11: 1-12); the universal prevalence of peace in the earth under the kingdom.

My* - (John 16:33-NIV Young Explorer's Bible) I have told you these things, so that in me you may have peace. In this world, you will have trouble. But take heart! I have overcome the world. (Col 3:15) Let the peace of Christ rule in your hearts, since as members of one body you were called to peace. And be thankful.

World* - (John 15:18-19) If the world hates you, keep in mind that it hated me first. If you belonged to the world, it would love you as its own. As it is, you do not belong to the world, but I have chosen you out of the world. That is why the world hates you. (John 7:7) The world cannot hate you, but it hates me because I testify that what it does is evil. (Rev 13:8 note) Cosmos, Summary: In the sense of the present world-system the ethically bad sense of the word, refers to the "order," "arrangement," under which Satan has organized the world of unbelieving mankind upon his cosmic principles of force, greed, selfishness, ambition, and pleasure (Mt 4:8-9; John 12:31; John 14:30; John 18:36; Eph 2:2; Eph 6:12; 1 John 2:15-17) This world-system is imposing and powerful with armies and fleets; is often outwardly religious, scientific, cultured, and elegant; but, seething with national and commercial rivalries and ambitions, is upheld in any real crisis only by armed force, and is dominated by Satanic principles.

Troubled* - (John 14:1) Do not let your hearts be troubled. Trust in God; trust also in me.

3. At this point, I have researched and written down the reference verses. I will reread the original Bible verse with this new knowledge. In my study journal, I will write my summary of what the verse means to me at the time.

131

4. I take time to reflect on the verse and the meaning.

Each verse has a different meaning for the individual, depending on what journey you are on at the time. You may read a verse one day and get a specific message, a month later, reading the same verse you receive a different message. That is the best example of why it is called the Living Bible.

As you spend time studying, your relationship with God will grow. Starting a Bible study, with the desire to strengthen or establish your relationship with God, I recommend starting with the Book of John. This book talks about God's love. Then continue with the Books of the Gospels: Matthew, Mark, and Luke.

Truthfully, anywhere you decide to begin is good. You will get wisdom from every book of the Bible.

Chapter 16 Reflection:

1. Do you have a study journal?

   _____

2. What is your favorite Book of the Bible?

   _____

   _____

   _____Why?

   _____

3. What is your favorite verse? _____

4. Why is it your favorite?_____

   _____

   _____

   _____

   _____

Part 4

Full of Blessings

Chapter 17

Blessings

Blessings are not only about income or toys but the level of life in which you want to live. Passing through the stages of life that take us to new levels is a lifelong pattern that is inescapable for those who pursue success. The only way to avoid starting at the bottom of a new level is to avoid success.

Life is composed of your thoughts, and your words construct it. If you do not like the life you are living, then change your thoughts. Thoughts determine conduct, character, and destiny, and therefore, your thoughts control your destiny. You alone are responsible for your thoughts – so plan wisely.

We release our creative energy through our words and thoughts. We are setting the world around us in motion. Our words frame our surroundings and thus build our lives. The thoughts you make and the words you use are the best tools for change in your life.

Remember: the only constant in maturing is changing. The most powerful thing in life is to create an image. The image is everything. The pictures in our mind determine our destiny. Dreams are the element of every great achievement in life. Dreams can die, vanish, or be stolen, but no person can live to their fullest potential without a desire to strive towards their vision. Thoughts are the substance of achievement.

The picture in your mind determines your future. The more specific the dream, the more influential the pull. A definite idea or dream creates hope, a sense of destiny, and purpose. A person without a vision is a person without a future. A person without a future will always return to his past.

Create a dream board. Gather pictures of the items you want in your life and put them on it. Look at it every moment you are able. Creating a dream board will help your subconscious focus on your desires, and they will begin to come into your life.

There are three significant requisites for success:

1. Plan wisely.
2. Use common sense.
3. Be resolute in what you know is right.

Fame can come in a moment, but greatness comes with longevity.

The dream is more important than individual roles. Write down what you would like to accomplish and a date, this could be one month, six months, years, or a specific time. Look over your goals daily and allow your subconscious to work on them. I do not mean to write them down and do not take the steps necessary to attain them but let your mind to work on them and start setting things in motion.

Chapter 17 Reflection:

1. Are your thoughts positive and encouraging?

   _____

2. What are your dreams?_____

   _____

   _____

3. Have you created a dream board?

   _____

   _____

4. What are the three requisites for success?

   _____

   _____

Chapter 18

Finances

Prosperous living is debt-free living, and managing debt is discipline.

Overcoming debt's harmful effects, we must become powerful enough to take a break from the culture around us. We need wisdom and strategy to break free, moving towards victory. It all starts with knowledge, then planning. The principles give us understanding; we develop the plan.

We achieve every stage of life incrementally.

Two giving principles:

1. Take care of the family.
2. Give to others

Remember that love is the desire to benefit others, even at your own expense. Let me clarify, you have $20, and want to purchase something that is not a necessity.

You notice a person on the street corner struggling, perhaps homeless. At that moment, you have a choice. Either give a portion of the money to help them or walk away. You may find yourself wanting to help but begin thinking 'they would probably make a poor decision with the money.' The gift here is allowing yourself to show unconditional love and in return feeling joy at helping another.

It does not matter what choice they make with the gift you have given-it is their free-will and by changing the method in which you give, you are taking away their free-will.

How much you care for others is the measure of your greatness. Answers for your needs will come through people. You qualify for more by how you deal with less.

- Invest in people. Investing is personal.
- Before investing in something financially, investigate, research.
- Risk do not gamble.
- It must be in writing. Write down your dreams and goals.
- If you lose an investment, do not hold onto regret; turn it over to the universe as a deposit for finances to come back to you exponentially.
- Shadows are fiercer than reality. Do not avoid reality because you are afraid of what others may think.
- Invest your life for your highest good. Any investment you make is always an investment of yourself.

You sow the future by what you reap from the past.

Learn to relate to others by learning to listen. You do not learn when you are always talking, you also do not hear and show concern and love for others when you do not pay attention.

Open your heart to those around you.

Tithing can seem overwhelming when you are not able to pay all your bills. You may be asking where do I find 10% of my income to give?

I struggled for quite some time on this; then it occurred to me – I was focusing only on the financial aspect of tithing. Yes, this is important, but you can tithe in other ways, as well. So, it is all about perspective!

You can tithe your time. When you donate old belongings, you are tithing. Remember the person on the street corner? You help them out; it is tithing. See where I am going with this?

Helping people, loving others – we receive wondrous rewards, along with help and love coming back to us.

Chapter 18 Reflection:

1. What are the two giving principles?

    _____

    _____

    _____

2. What should you invest in?

    _____

    _____

    _____

3. What should you do if you lose an investment?

    _____

    _____

    _____

4. You relate to others by:

    _____

    _____

    _____

About the Author

Ashleigh Benson is a Teacher, Counselor, Spiritual Coach, and Minister. She helps individuals and organizations access a more fulfilling life through self-development.

Ashleigh has struggled with significant loss and finding a profound purpose for her life. Losing her 24-year-old daughter, she was able to transform her grief into helping and encouraging others to have a life full of meaning and potential. She has been blessed with three exceptional children and lives near Reno, NV.

Ashleigh has been in many leadership roles throughout her journey. She was a Preschool and Children's Director, where she oversaw the teaching and nurturing of the children. Ashleigh has been a Women's Director, coaching, counseling, and leading Bible studies. She was a Vacation Bible Study Director for four years, igniting spiritual growth in both children and teachers; during this time, attendance went from fifty children to over 250. She has spoken to groups about struggle and growth through life experiences in several churches.

She was a Counselor and Staff Director for Diabetes Camps for five years, teaching children how to manage their diabetes and have fun even with this disability.

Ashleigh believes in teaching by example and creating dynamic teams.

www.ingramcontent.com/pod-product-compliance
Lightning Source LLC
Chambersburg PA
CBHW070825100426
42813CB00003B/498